# ESTABLISH ME

JAMES C. NYEMAH

Forte Publishing

FORTE Publishing

First Published in 2016
Published by:
**FORTE** Publications
#12 Ashmun Street
Snapper Hill
Monrovia, Liberia

**FORTE** Publishing
7202 Tavenner Lane
# 208 Alexandria
VA, 22306

**FORTE** Press
76 Sarasit Road
Ban Pong, 70110
Ratchaburi, Thailand

http://fortepublishing.wix.com/fppp

ISBN:
ISBN-13:

# DEDICATION

I dedicate this book to all the pastors in Liberia, West Africa, especially to the great pastors in Monrovia, Zwedru, Pleebo, Harper and its environs; to all the great men and women on the frontline who keep the fire of the gospel burning. To all the pastors and leaders whose courage has helped me over the years to fulfill my purpose in conducting leadership conferences across Liberia.

I give special honor to my pastors, pastors of the great church Africa Faith Expressions – Rev. J. Robertson Cooper in Harper and Pastor Frederick Youbie in Pleebo. I really want to appreciate all the family and the great people at my home church in Phoenix, Arizona – USA. You rock! You are so tough in the Lord that my absence did not make the people of God miss a thing. You are so tough in the Lord that my absence does not make the people of God to miss a thing. You picked up the cross and continued ministry in my constant absence. I really thank God for your strong leadership, prayer and support. You are not like the other people who took advantage of our generosity and broke away from the church and caused us a lot of problems. May the God I serve bless you in every way. I thank God for your faith in me as your leader. I can see the Lord doing great things in you and taking you from one level to the other in due time. Hold fast to your calling and do not let anything rob you of your prize in glory.

And, to Rev. Joseph Wholubah in Pleebo and Rev. Victor Nyonsiea in Zwedru and all the other great pastors for your efforts toward the Leadership Conferences held between 2011 and 2013. To my own man, Rev. Abilio Balboa, Resident Pastor of the Philadelphia Central Church in Congo Town, Monrovia, I say thank you RP! And, to Rev. Jimmy

Kuoh, General Superintendent - Emeritus, of the Liberia Assemblies of God Church, for your astute leadership in mobilizing all the pastors of the Assemblies of God Church in Grand Gedeh and Maryland area to be a part of the leadership conferences. Thank you.

Can I really do this without recognizing one special person? No, I do not think so. There is one special minister, one special woman of God, of course that is Licentiate Rachel Brown, my own mother at the Philadelphia Central Church! This woman loves to pray. I am sorry that Bishop Harris made you to follow me around in Liberia. I still remember you screaming telling me to slow down when I was driving fast on the rough roads between Monrovia and Pleebo. I can never forget that. While you were right about my high speed, it was so funny to me. I love you mama for all you are doing. Thank you!

And, to the only person, the only enabling body, even the Holy Spirit for manifesting in us the glory of the LORD in every area of the ministry in Liberia – thank you! I could not do anything without you. You put the Word in my spirit. You bore witness and brought us in partnership for fulfillment. Sometimes I felt inadequate, but you gave me courage, and partners, and resources, and testimonies! Thank you LORD!

.

# CONTENTS

Contents

# Acknowledgments

It is a great honor to know all the special men and women in my life who assist me in many ways as I journey to prominence; thank you. One of those special people is my own man, D. Othniel Forte, the brain behind Liberian Literary Magazine, who, through his encouragement, prompted me to write this book. More than just fellow authors, we are now partners to expand literacy in our home country Liberia, and to put our country on the international scene for producing prolific authors.

I really want to thank my family, my wife and daughter, for your confidence in me and your constant prayers. I thank God for my church and all those who support me. I thank all my readers around the world and all my fans on social networks. You are the ones who give me the courage to write more books as the Lord puts them in my spirit; get ready to read more and be blessed. I promise to bring you the best of me, not just to make you feel good, but to give you something that will help make you and better you. Thank you.

I thank God for my son, my spiritual son, William *Mr. Breakthrough* Fannoh and his wife, Theresa, for staying with me in long hours of daily prayer. You will reap your rewards right here and up in glory. The Lord will take you to places and change your address. I can see great things the Lord will do in you. Get ready!

# Part One

**PART 1**: **The Sin that Easily Entangles**

# The Sin that Easily Entangles

*Can two walk together unless they have agreed to do so?* **Amos 3:3 NIV**

Nowadays we do not hear pastors preaching on the topics of sin, repentance, holiness and righteous living or judgment; instead, we hear crowd-moving sermons on blessings, forgiveness, restoration and money. However, the sad truth is that even if God forgives you of your sin but you do not repent and start to live a holy and righteous life, the effects of sin will riddle your life with troubles.

That is why many people who have been in church for a long time are still not happy and never advance – because the wages of sin is death! Not just physical death alone; death can come in your finances – while others are doing great things with money, you could be broke and struggling in poverty, trying to make it from one paycheck to the other without realizing anything good.

Death could come in your relationships, too, and you will find no happiness. In fact, some people never find real love – they do not find anyone to love them enough to marry them. Yet many of them go to their friends' weddings from place to place, sometimes acting as if it were their wedding.

Death, because of sin, can show its ugly face in every aspect of your life if you do not come clean before God. There is no other way to jump over the penalty of sin apart from the redemptive work of the Lord Jesus Christ. Therefore, we need to make a response to God and say yes to him and allow him to take our lives and do something better.

The other crowd-pleasing messages we often hear about from the pulpit are prophecy, healing, deliverance and, of course, miracles! When a pastor preaches about financial blessings, about how God will bless people with money, cars and houses, and then tell church members to give money in the form of a seed, people rush to the altar and give from what they do not have in the hopes of getting something better from God. Many people end up in regret for giving their last money to the pastor because nothing can change.

They forget to understand that God wants you more than he wants your stuff. They forget that you cannot bribe God with things so that he will help you while you continue to be a rebellious child. God wants you, not just your money and other stuff. It does not work like that.

People run here and there for prophecies, like those who run to tarot cards and palm readers or psychics. What is prophecy if it does not benefit your life and benefit the church of the living God?

Why is it that people are anxious to hear somebody tell stories about their lives and sometimes instill fear? Sometimes I wonder if pastors told people their ugly secrets, especially in public, whether they would ever go to that church or meeting again. People run after prophets and pastors because of prophesies instead of running after God!

Sadly, many prophets, bishops, apostles and pastors want notoriety; they want to make a name for themselves instead of preaching and teaching God's word. Pastors need to declare the truth about the Word of God and not just become crowd-pleasers and moneymakers.

Discussion of the issue of sin seems forbidden in some churches. Some pastors never preach about sins because they will be preaching against themselves. They are high-class sinners, dressed in nice clothes and toting Bibles in their hands. They talk big about God, but they do not really have any relationship with God. They do not experience the joy of the Lord, and neither have they known the peace that comes from living for God. All they do is to put up shows to fool the crowd.

Other pastors give people a blank check to live any way they want because the blood of Jesus Christ paid for sins, so it does not matter what anyone does these days. Wow, I wish that were true! The teachings on sin, holiness and righteousness seem to have been only for the early believers, not for modern Christians today. It somehow sounds like those believers never knew much about Christ's redemptive work the way our biblical scholars, theologians, and even pastors, bishops, apostles, prophets and pastors know God today.

Today's clergy seem to have some *"new revelation"* that nullifies the work of the cross, changes the language of holiness and righteous and focuses only on the benefits of this salvation, playing down the requirements.

The funny part is that pastors like to assume many prestigious offices of the Christian Church except that of the evangelist. I think the reasons are obvious. The work of the evangelist is to preach salvation, repentance of sins, forgiveness of God and of self, to implement the ordinances of water baptisms and Holy Communion, to promote holiness and righteousness because we are the temple of the Living God.

All such messages will make one surrender to self and let God receive them, forgive and transform them and build them up into the One Holy Church that affects change in the world.

Such messages talk about our response, our requirement and our obligation to God; they bring about the issue of accountability. People have misunderstood accountability and take it as judgment – the two are different, though accountability could bring judgment. God takes the issue of sin seriously. Because of sin, Christ came to die on the cross for us; it is not a good thing for anybody who claims to be a Christian to dishonor his sacrifice for us. God does not want us to live in sin. He wants all of us to come from out of sin and receive grace to become better people.

## a. PUT ASIDE THE SIN

There is a call to salvation for everyone who cares to listen. This call is indiscriminate in every sense of the word because everyone can receive salvation regardless of race, age or socio-economic status. The call to salvation extends to all peoples everywhere, and that includes you and me. The Bible teaches us that there is a savior who can take away our sins and wash us as white as snow. Jesus Christ is the savior! Sometimes in the past, I really wondered if God can truly take away all sins because of how terrible and wicked some people can be; especially the wickedness beyond words they have done to other people.

Quite interestingly, I have come to understand that the answer is a shocking "yes!" Even if people do things for which the state gives them capital punishment, whether lifetime imprisonment or the death penalty, God can still forgive their sins if they confess and repent. This, to me, is something powerful about the love of God that covers all our sins.

Inasmuch as God is willing to forgive sinners, there is a condition – confess and repent. The Apostle Paul makes it clear to everyone that we cannot continue in sin and somehow expect grace to cover us. It does not work. If we continue in sin, the penalty of sin can catch us; and that is not something we really want.

[1]*What then? Shall we sin because we are not under the law but under grace? Certainly not! Do you not know that to whom you present yourselves slaves to obey, you are that one's slaves who you obey, whether of sin leading to death, or of obedience leading to righteousness?* **Romans 6:15-16 NKJV**

The truth remains that we make ourselves obligated to people and things. Yet one question remains: to whom and to what? We can decide to obey God and follow his commands. When we do so, in spite of our weaknesses, the Lord has a way of lifting us up and giving us the abundant life. Living for God is not easy, but it is quite rewarding. The journey can get tough at times, but the Lord promised to be there always. Only those who dare obey God can know and understand that there is power in the Word of God; let that be you today.

After you have received salvation, if pastors tell you that you can sin scar-free, with no consequences, I am sorry for you because those pastors lie to you. Sin brings death – physical, emotional, mental and spiritual. The pain of sin is terrible. Some of the pain is visible. Nevertheless, the deep emotional and mental pain that sin can bring can be quite devastating. People have killed others or committed suicide because of the results of sin. I have seen children suffer because of sin. I have seen the bad and sorrowful things sin can bring. Sin causes problems in every area of life.

Many pretty girls have died or lost their way because of sin. Sin has killed rich and powerful people. Many boys are roaming around looking for what they have lost because of sin. They have lost their way to leadership and have become followers.

Sin has caused the guilty and the innocent to suffer in prisons worldwide. Sin has killed so many innocent babies through abortion. Sin has killed plenty of people and cheated families because of drunk driving, gambling, drugs and the gangster life. Sin has caused wars in medieval times and modern times, even today. Sin has caused wars in Africa and the Middle East; while brothers and brothers are killing each other, strangers are looting their land and laughing at their misery. Sin has caused financial institutions, including banks, to steal millions from people, caused recessions and destabilized world markets. Sin has caused the rich and powerful to invent killing machines like poisonous vaccines causing terrible diseases including infanticide, drug-induced barrenness and many horrible diseases.

In addition, of course, sin has killed millions of poor people. I want to ask you a question: Would you stand by God's word and live a holy and righteous life, or would you let some unruly ignorant and rebellious pastor wrongly interpret the Word of God to fit his or her selfish desires and lead you astray? I pray for all these false pastors with big titles who are bereft of the grace of God to change or face the wrath of God. They blindly lead thousands of people astray.

The funny part of this is that church members love pastors who lie to them, steal their money, sleep with them, drink and party in secret. They let the pastors give them special favors in return for the gross sin committed against them. They are more concerned about earthly things than the treasures up in glory; they want all the blessings and rewards right now, right here on earth. It appears somehow that there is some truth in their actions; because they will not enter heaven, they would rather get their payment right here. Instead of craving the true Word of God, they follow sweet-sounding pastors who know how to brainwash people, pastors who are nothing but scammers. Wicked pastors master the art of leading people astray without their knowledge and robbing them of the benefits of being a part of the kingdom of God. The Bible teaches us in the book of Hebrews that we should put aside the sin that easily entangles, the sin that weighs us down, ensnares us and destroys our lives. The Lord calls us to put aside sin and relieve ourselves of every weight it brings.

*²Therefore, since we are surrounded by such a great cloud of witnesses, let us throw off everything that hinders and the sin that so easily entangles. And let us run with perseverance the race marked out for us, fixing our eyes on Jesus, the pioneer and perfecter of faith. For the joy set before him he endured the cross, scorning its shame, and sat down at the right hand of the throne of God.* **Hebrews 12:1-2 NIV**

We have witnesses everywhere; a cloud of witnesses surrounds us everywhere we go. The witnesses report everything that happens; that means both good and bad things. We have people and angels monitoring us; we need to do our best to present ourselves the best way possible everywhere we go. We need to be very careful because sin hinders and sin easily entangles. Sin traps. Sin destroys even if you are alive; sin can make you look like a corpse walking around.

Looking at the gravity of the situation sin brings, we need to persevere and run the race of life marked for us. Each one of us has our own race in life, a path to follow. We need to fix our eyes on Jesus Christ; he is the author and finisher of our faith. Our salvation starts with Jesus and ends with Jesus, so we need to keep our eyes on Jesus Christ. Regardless of what struggles we have in the Christian faith, the Lord wants us to hold onto him, to hold onto his unchanging hands.

Many people today want to go on in life, even Christians, without Jesus Christ. The Bible encourages us to endure the pains of being a follower of Jesus Christ and then we can share in his glory. Sadly, these days, nobody seems willing to lay down his or life for God, but somehow they want all the things from the kingdom of God for free.

They do not really want God, but they want things from God. In addition, because of the things they want from God, some of them do not mind joining a church, not because they want God, but because they want blessings. Moreover, if God gives them blessings, they continue in their sins, holding onto them with one hand and two feet, with the other hand in the church to receive miracles.

John the Revelator tells us that we need to confess our sins and God will be faithful in his promises to us.

> *[3]If we claim to be without sin, we deceive ourselves and the truth is not in us. If we confess our sins, he is faithful and just and will forgive us our sins and purify us from all unrighteousness.* **I John 1:8-9 NIV**

The first thing here is that no lie goes free in the presence of God. We cannot claim perfection or righteousness without God; righteousness comes from the Lord. We need to give a response to God and not fool ourselves. On the other hand, if we come to terms with ourselves and recognize our weaknesses and our sins, the Lord is faithful in his word to forgive and cleanse us from all unrighteousness. To me, this is good news for everyone; this is good news for every sinner.

The good news says that God can forgive us regardless of what we have done and give us another chance in life. All we have to do is to respond to God. The Prophet Isaiah talks about the ordeal of sinners and the response of our loving God.

> *[4]"Come now, let us reason together, "says the LORD, "Though your sins are like scarlet, they shall be as white as snow; though they are red like crimson, they shall be as wool. If you are willing and obedient, you shall eat the good of the land; but if you refuse and rebel, you shall be devoured by the sword"; for the mouth of the Lord has spoken.* **Isaiah 1: 18-19 NKJV**

God calls all the sinners to come to a meeting; it is a serious discussion about sin because it destroys our relationship with him. The topic of discussion is sin, sin and sin. In the discussion, God assures sinners that everyone can count on his promises, that he can forgive, restore, sanctify and bless sinners only if they are willing and obedient. He goes on to further describe sin in its magnitude; whether it is black as scarlet or red as crimson, he can blot it out completely for eternity. The only requirement is true repentance.

Meanwhile, there is a clause in the deal that protects the interest of God; it says that we must do something. It is a unique clause that says that everyone must do things the way God wants them by simply obeying him. He said that if we are willing and obedient, we shall eat the good of the land. On the other hand, our unwillingness and disobedience will make us guilty in the judgment of God. The sword is ready to destroy all disobedient souls. God does not want us to be rebels in this world. The way to become a rebel is to say no to God and to his plan of salvation for us. It is saying yes to the evils in this world as we treat one another badly and destroy our planet. It is my prayer that all of us will say yes to God so that our lives can become better, and together we will make a better world full of peace and tranquility.

## b. SIN DESTROYS

Sin destroys; this I know very well. I almost destroyed my life because of my own sins. I almost destroyed my life because I let the sins of other people mess me up. My life was almost messed up because of the sin in the community and society as a whole. Sin destroys. I know quite well that sin destroys, and the destruction varies in size and magnitude. It brings big shame and small shame. It destroys individuals, families, friends, people groups, nations and the world.

Inasmuch as some sinful things can be enjoyable, the result is not always good. It is like eating sugar. Though sugar is sweet, a lot of sugar can make you sick. Drugs may seem fun, but they affect your thinking ability and judgment. Sexual immorality can be fun, but the unplanned pregnancies, abortions, failed marriages and sicknesses are not fun at all.

The Bible describes the enemy as a thief who comes in to steal, kill and destroy.

*⁵The thief does not come except to steal, and to kill, and to destroy. I have come that they may have life, and that they may have it more abundantly.* **John 10:10 NKJV**

The devil uses sin to steal your future, kill your dreams and aspirations, and destroy your destiny. Repeatedly we have seen how the devil skillfully destroys the lives of our youth by giving them wrong ambitions. He steals their lives and gives them false enjoyment through the party life, drugs, alcohol, the gangster life and sex. As they are caught up in that, their chance to become leaders on the world stage is minimized if not eliminated. The devil knows how to trap people by suggesting duplicates of the original things God planned for us. The devil shows us so-called shortcuts in life: a way to get us in serious trouble and remove us from the scene of the world-changers. I feel bad every time I see a life being destroyed by Satan, whether it is a child, a young person or an adult. It is a pitiful thing.

Sin is the common yet powerful weapon of the enemy. Because the devil knows that sin separates us from God, he uses that and then deals us the last blow by destroying everything about us. Meanwhile, if we are not careful, the devil will turn us into wicked people to carry out his commands to destroy other innocent lives. One of the terrible ways that sin destroys is that it separates us from God. Any soldier who is separated from the team is open to enemy attacks or capture if he or she is not careful. A child who is separated from his or her parents, even at a ball game or in the streets, can suffer loneliness. When we are separated from God, we become very vulnerable, and the enemy can use the opportunity to turn us into his punching bag.

> *⁶Behold, the Lord's hand is not shortened, that it cannot save; nor his ear heavy that it cannot hear. But your iniquities have separated you from your God; and your sins have hidden his face from you, so that he will not hear.* **Isaiah 59:1-2 NKJV**

The Prophet Isaiah rightly says that God is not lazy, blind or deaf. He is alive, active and powerful. He is able to fulfill his Word concerning us. Each one of us needs to follow the requirements of the Lord by responding to the call of salvation, something free of charge. Do not let anyone fool you when it comes to the issue of sin; sin actually destroys. If this were not a big deal, Jesus Christ would not have come down and died a vicarious death on the cross – something so horrible, just for you and me. If sin were nothing in the eyes of God, Jesus Christ would not have been rejected by his own people and received such a horrendous beating from the

Roman soldiers. He suffered and died a terrible death so that his blood could pay the price of sin. Now you tell me, are you going to let yourself or someone else fool you and overlook the salvation of God?

There is a growing trend in the church that is very ridiculous. Pastors are guilty as much as church members. It is the issue of putting sacrifice over obedience. People want to give to God, to do things for God, even sacrifice for God, but they do not really want to do what God asks them to do by living for him. The deception of the devil permeates the modern church; this deception says that one can be a Christian without living for God. It causes us to lose our position in God. This, for some people, could lead to death – our own death and the deaths of our family and friends! King Samuel, the first king of Israel, learned this lesson the hard way. Sadly, he did not live to tell the story. He and his sons died in battle the same day as the Prophet Samuel spoke.

> [7]So Samuel said: "Has the Lord as great delight in burnt offerings and sacrifices, as in obeying the voice of the Lord? Behold, to obey is better than sacrifice, and to heed than the fat of rams. Now Samuel said to Saul, "Why have you disturbed me bring bringing me up?" Moreover, the Lord will also deliver Israel with you into the hand of the Philistines. And tomorrow you and your sons will be with me. The Lord will also deliver the army of Israel into the hand of the Philistines."
> **SAMUEL 15:22, 28:15 & 19 NKJV**

The sin of King Saul was offering sacrifice instead of waiting for Prophet Samuel; keeping the king alive and bringing livestock led to his untimely demise. He rebelled against the Word of the Lord by sparing the life of the king, bringing in cattle and offering sacrifice, something only the prophet was supposed to do. All these sins were the result of disobedience.  Because he disobeyed, the Lord stopped talking to him; because of a pending war, desperate King Saul used a witch medium to invoke the spirit of the late Prophet Samuel.  The sin of disobedience and doing things only a prophet should do made God reject him as king, even though he refused to step down.  The sin of consulting a medium to talk to the late prophet led to his death.  Instead of King Saul dying alone, he and all his sons died, including our beloved Jonathan; and the army of Israel perished at the hands of the Philistines, as the prophet has said.

I want to be clear with you.  Please get rid of that sin which easily entangles.  Please get rid of that secret sin before it becomes public.  Please get rid of that sin before it destroys you and other innocent people, even the good people connected to you, like what happened to Jonathan.  Sin separates.  Sin destroys.  Do not let sin destroy you and your family and friends.  Sin actually destroys.  Beware!

## c. HOPE FOR THE SINNER

I am so grateful to the Lord that there is hope for the sinner: the hope that says that no matter what you have done, the Lord can accept you, forgive you and even restore you. To me, this is the best thing for any sinner to hear. When I think about my own weaknesses, the bad things I did before, the secret and shameful things, and when I know that the Lord is willing to fix me up – I love that! I must be very grateful to God for the offer. This offer has only one simple condition – my willingness to come and reason with God. I will take that any time, any day! I know what I have done. I know where I have been. I know the secrets I do not want anybody to know. I know the embarrassing things I did; yes, I know what I have done.

However, to know that the Lord can truly forgive me, cleanse me from all my sins and restore me, is the best thing to know. I want that for my friends, all my family members and everyone else. This salvation is good for me and everybody I know. I know what some of them and I did together. For me, my response is simple – yes, Lord! There is nothing to think about, nothing to postpone because I am tired of the situation that sin has brought upon me. I know what I did and what it brought upon my life. I know the constant reminders I hate so much. I see the scars. I know the emotional trauma. I know the pain.

That is why, without any reservations or remorse, I step out of the line, raise my hands up to heaven and say, "Lord, I surrender all to you today." I surrender my mind. This mind of mine can cause problems by thinking about weird things. Instead of thinking about principal things, it is sometimes embarrassing to say what comes into my mind. I hate that. I surrender my heart because as simple as forgiveness is, sometimes I even find it hard to forgive. As sweet as love is, I struggle to love people at times. Yet I know deep down in my heart that if I need the forgiveness of God and of others, I too must forgive those who trespass against me. I surrender my body to God – all of it. Sometimes my body calls for pleasures for which I should not be asking. This is so sad.

I need God to transform my life and make it into something wonderful. With all my flaws, I believe there is something good about me that God can use, or at least something he can fix. I need God to conform my will to that of the Lord Jesus Christ. I need to be resolute in doing what the Lord pleases. I need my heart to change so that it can be soft and nice. I have come to understand that from the abundance of the heart, my mouth speaks, so I want to control my mouth; I need to sanction my heart right away.

I need God. I need God today. I need God every day of my life. I cannot waste any valuable time for the rest of my life. I want God now. I want to take the offer now before something else happens and things change for me. I have not lost my body to sickness, or lost my life to jail time or to some other predicament, so I would rather come free of charge to God today before the price changes. I like the offer. Listen to what the Prophet Isaiah has to say.

*[8] "Come now, and let us reason together," Says the Lord, "Though your sins are like scarlet, they shall be as white as snow; though they are red like crimson, they shall be as wool. If you are willing and obedient, you shall eat the good of the land. But if you refuse and rebel, you shall be devoured by the sword." For the mouth of the Lord has spoken.* **Isaiah 1: 18-20 NKJV**

What I really love about this passage is that it makes a unique offer to everyone: the offer to come to God and reason with him. Instead of God exacting hellfire judgment upon us, we receive a call for discussion to fix our sin problem. I am so grateful to God for his call. In my weakness, when people call me out, it is not usually for discussion like this; they can state my wrongdoing as it is and blast the devil out of me and condemn my actions harshly. Unlike this, God, in his compassion and loving kindness, offers me a seat to discuss. For me to even approach the throne room as a sinner is a hard thing, yet interestingly I have to learn to trust in his word and come anyway. I can see that there is a place to hang things. Oh no, that place is not for overcoats; it is the cross where I can drop all the weight, all the pain, all my sins, and then approach the father.

At first, looking at my sins and weaknesses, I thought it was a death trap; but no, it is a place of salvation. Whoosh, I thank God that I can approach! The Lord tells me that no matter what my sins are, if they are dark as scarlet, whether secretive, or red as crimson, and public, he can wash them as white as snow. He can clear me of all the guilt and the penalty of death. All I have to do is accept the offer and surrender all to the Lord. I must turn from my wicked ways and sins and allow the transformation of life to take its course in me. My pace may not be the same as yours, but I am in my master's hands and he is working on me day by day.

It says that if you and I are willing and obedient, we will eat of the good of the land. Wow! He was talking about the remission of our sins and now the talk jumps all the way to restoration and commission. Not only will he wash us as white as snow, but if we are willing and obedient, he will give us the good things of the land. He will put us in charge of other people and things. We will eat our portion and take care of the rest. I love that!

As good as this deal sounds, there is the second portion of which we must be very careful. The second part says that if we refuse the deal and continue to rebel, we will be cut off. Ouch! Yes, it says our refusal would be detrimental to us. It could cause us death – physical, emotional, mental and spiritual death! God is the author and finisher of everything, including our faith. He is the one who gives and takes life. Because of this, we must take his Word very seriously. When God says something, he means it; his offer has life and death – let us choose wisely.

I have seen many folks struggle, suffer and die because they have refused the offer of God; please do not let that happen to you. We have a choice to say yes to God, to live and enjoy the good of the land. Such harsh punishment is not really for you and me; all we have to do to escape it is to give our lives to the Lord and live for him. Look, I believe that you and I can do better. You can get out of that mess and live a better life. I can overcome the sin, too. Let us do this together. I am ready; I hope you are ready, too.

## d. BECOME NEW AGAIN

You and I can become new again; I love that so much. Wow, that is good news! Many times people look at God as an angry, disgruntled man who is ready to zap us for our sins and failures. Some people see God as the person who makes impossible demands just so he can punish us. Because of this, we blame God for every evil imaginable that happens to us and in our society. Inasmuch as we can do whatever we want, we need to understand that if our actions are creating problems for us, our families and society, we need to repent. The good news is that the enabling power of God can renew us; it is a great thing to know. I am so glad to know that.

When we answer the call of God to come and reason with him, part of the package we get is to become a new creation. God cleanses us of all our sins and makes us brand new. Let me tell you this: it is the best experience in the world to see the weight of sin and its punishment lifted off our shoulders. God takes us back to our original state of righteousness: a place of purity not gained by works, but by faith. He takes us to a position in which we can talk with God as children and friends.

The Apostle Paul, in a special letter to the church in Corinth, wrote about salvation and the remission of sins when he said,

*⁹Therefore, if anyone is in Christ, he is a new creation; old things have passed away; behold, all things have become new.* **2 CORINTHIANS 5:17 NKJV**

There has been a lot of talk in the church world about whether we could lose our salvation. Some people argued about whether we really need to follow the statutes of the Lord because the death of Christ paid for our sins. I see that many Christians today want to be Christians, but they do not want to change their lifestyles. They want to dwell in their sins because the death of Jesus paid for our sins today and in the future. It is as if someone gave us a blank check to cash without caution. Just because Jesus died for our sins does not mean that we do not honor his death; we cannot manipulate Scriptures to fit our warped minds because we love to live in sin.

The Apostle Paul clearly states that if anyone is in Christ, he or she is a new creation. I want to tell all the people who are proud of their sins, and especially those who lead others astray by preaching false doctrines, that without the transformation to a new creation, we are not actually born again. We only responded mentally or emotionally; it did not come from our hearts, so we never made any changes in our lives. To become a new creation, there has to be a total change of mind, heart and life. We must become new people. We must repent of our sins and live holy and righteous lives. We must be born again before we can enjoy our access to the hope God has given us.

The Bible teaches us that without holiness, no one will see God. Do not let any pastor, family member or friend lie to you, saying that you can just live like that and go free.

*[10]Pursue peace with all people, and holiness, without which no one will see the Lord.* **Hebrews 12:14 NKJV**

If we want to see God, we need to live a holy and righteous life and be at peace with others. We must put aside all the grudges we keep. We must begin to speak to all the people from whom we kept speech. We need to put aside every evil hidden in our hearts and minds, and put on holiness and righteous.

*[11]"But the righteous one will live by faith. And I take no pleasure in the one who shrinks back."* **Hebrews 10:38 NKJV**

I know someone might be thinking, 'This is so impossible, looking at the depraved world we live in today.' No, no my friend; remember, it is not by our might, but by the spirit of the Lord. It is not solely by human works; it is by faith. We must begin to exercise our faith in the Lord and solely depend on him. It is not about our righteousness, but His righteousness. All we have to do is to apply faith. The Lord takes our lives, molds them and makes them something better. All we have to do to become the new creation is trust and obey God. We may not have the strength, but he does. We may not know how, but he knows everything. We must not try to play God, but rather allow God to be God and we remain his beloved children and friends. When we live by faith, all things become possible because the God we serve controls all things.

> *[12]Jesus looked at them and said, "With man this is impossible, but with God all things are possible."* **Matthew 19:26 NIV**

To live for God is not easy; I am not going to lie to you, but it is the best thing in the world to do. The problem many Christians have is that they want to live for God on their own strength and understanding. It does not work. We must learn to trust and obey God.

> *[13]Trust in the Lord with all your heart and lean not on your own understanding; in all your ways submit to him, and he will make your paths straight. Do not be wise in your own eyes; fear the Lord and shun evil. This will bring health to your body and nourishment to your bones.* **Proverbs 3: 5-8 NIV**

Jesus, speaking to Nicodemus, a member of the Jewish ruling council and a man who was expected to know the Word of God but who did not know the truth, said:

*[14]Jesus answered and said to him, "Most assuredly, I say to you, unless one is born again, he cannot see the kingdom of God." Nicodemus said to Him, "How can a man be born when he is old? Can he enter a second time into his mother's womb and be born? Most assuredly, I say to you, unless one is born of water and the Spirit, he cannot enter the kingdom of God. That which is born of the flesh is flesh, and that which is born of the Spirit is spirit. Do not marvel that I said to you, 'You must be born again.' The wind blows where it wishes, and you hear the sound of it, but cannot tell where it comes from and where it goes. So is everyone who is born of the Spirit.* **John 3:3-5 NKJV**

Unless you are born again, you cannot see the kingdom of God, much less enter it; this blows out the ego of so many people who like the easy way out. Jesus told old Nicodemus that it is not about our physical strength or personal ideas; it is a matter of the Spirit. We must be born again, born of water and of the Spirit. We have to do things God's way, not our way.

We must receive the free gift of salvation and walk the walk, not just talk and act religious. It is not about how many Bible verses pastors can quote. It is not about how people speak in tongues, not about just prophesies and miracles; it is about living correctly for God. What will it do for you to dress like true believers, go to church like them, talk like them, do things like them, but yet your heart and soul are not in it? It is like going to swim in the river or ocean and expecting yourself to turn into a fish just because you swam. It does not work like that. You must be born again; I must be born again to receive the hope for repented sinners.

When I was much younger, I did not understand what benefit Christians got from keeping all these straight rules from God. Today I have come to realize that I am what I am because of my faith; otherwise, youthful passions would have torn my life apart. There was a time when I was not really into the things of God as I am now; but even during that time, I knew the difference between those with the title of Christians and those who were actually born again.

Born-again believers' prayer was very powerful. They carry a certain spirit, a certain connection with God that others did not possess. They got revelations that some makeshift pastors did not have, but they were just ordinary church members with no positions or titles in the church. They prayed. They worshiped. They gave. They believed. And they were truly powerful in representing God wherever they went.

There were other Christians who did not go to church very often, but we would see them in social gatherings. They complained about the Praise Team, about how they sang the same old songs. They complained about how long the pastor preached. They complained about how the church was asking people for money every time, even though they did not give their tithes and offerings. Their activities in the church can tell you how prayerless their lives were, so no need to talk about that. They had no weight, no power; definitely, they did not connect to God in a way that someone else could feel.

The truth is, people know how serious we are in the things of the Lord. God has given us hope to restore and commission us. We can let go of the past and hold on to a new and bright future. Let me be quick to say this: inasmuch as we can look at other Christians to encourage ourselves in the Lord, our faith in God should not be based solely on what others do, though we serve the same God. The Christian faith is a personal decision every person need to make. Not by compulsion, not by anything else; we come to God because we understand that we need God in our lives.

Christians who are born again, born of water and of the Spirit, are quite interesting. Once you see one, you will know because there is a certain magnet in them that pulls people toward them. That magnet is the Spirit of the Lord. It is contagious. It is powerful. People who are true born-again believer have lives that are so interesting. It is not that they have everything in this world, but they have the peace and joy of the Lord. They simply trust God for everything they need in life. They are not depressed about money, cars, houses, family and things like that; they depend on God to provide and build them up. From day to day, they grow in faith, experience the daily mercies of God and enjoy his grace.

I want to encourage you, my dear friend, to try God and surrender all to him. There is a force stronger than you are that wants to destroy your life, but the Lord has a way for you. Regardless of what you have done, the Lord wants to forgive you if you are willing and repent. When you do so, the Lord promises to forgive you, to wash you clean and give you a bright future. I really encourage you to try God; you will discover that he is all right. When I see how God can deliver prostitutes, gangbangers, crooks, murderers, witches, wicked people and ordinary sinners, it tells me that God is truly loving and compassionate. His plan is not to give you impossible rules so that he can catch and punish you. No, the rules he gives are guidelines to help us stay in our lane on the freeway of life. Life has traps and evil schemes, but following the way of God will help you and me navigate all the difficult paths of life, fulfill our purpose and reach our destiny.

God has a bright future for you. I look forward to hearing about the goodness of God in your life. Your parents expect something good of you. Your family and friends count on you. Moreover, your society is looking for people like you to make a difference. People are looking for someone like you to take that leadership role that will put you on the platform to serve others. I believe that when you say yes to God, surrender to him, you will experience your best life to date.

Please do not let anyone fool you into saying that God does not care about what we do once we have become Christians; this is a lie. We cannot remain the same, do the same things and expect everything to be good between God and us. God is only moved by what we give him, not just what we say. It is so easy to talk, and many of us know how to do that quite well. I encourage you today to give everything to God so that you can have life in abundance. Be born again and experience the true power of true believers. When you do, you will not want to go back to that old stuff. I look forward to hearing about how the Lord is going to do great things in your life. Let go of the sin that easily entangles and say yes to God. God wants to establish you, but you have to settle the sin problem that separates you from him. May God give you all the grace you need to get out of any situation that prevents you from having a meaningful relationship with Him. May He establish you in grace to prosper in all your ways and become all you can be. Thank you.

# Part Two

## PART 2: The Power of Service

a. Serving Clergy and Officials
b. Church Leaders
c. Serving People, Even Lay People
d. Equally Rewarded
e. Service Takes Sacrifice
f. Service, Not Personal Gain
g. Selfish Ambition Stirs Up /Strife
h. Good Service, Not Eye-Service

# The Power of Service

There is something very powerful about service that many people do not know or overlook. One of the greatest things we have that steers our world in the marketplace, whether in goods and services, or in the church, and many other disciplines of life is, the power of good service. I hate being ignored at the counter in stores when I go buy something. I really hate being talked to rough by clerks in offices and ushers or event staffs when I go to games or concerts. It is not funny at all. Even if they have some problems that creates delay, I would appreciate if someone would just tell me what is going on, then I will know what to do.

Good customer service is in demand everywhere. We need good customer service in every area of life; we just need people to talk to us nicely, show us proper respect as we do business with their companies, organizations or groups. To show proper honor to people to whom it is due can be powerful and rewarding; whether it is our parents, teachers, pastors, and other leaders, we need to show respect others and diligently serve them.

In the power of service, you will discover that the better you serve people with dignity, the more they will do business with you and go beyond the requirement. If you talk to people good and treat them nicely, they will give you their loyalty and it becomes a "win, win" situation. It is my hope that after you read this section, you will begin to take service seriously in any discipline of life you find yourself in.

## a. SERVING CLERGY AND OFFICIALS

One of the most misused Scriptures when it comes to receiving blessings from God is the one below. Christians like to say that their God will provide all their needs according to his riches in glory. Yet, when you look at them, they do not look like people who have been collecting riches from up in glory. Many of them are broke, sick and poor.

What they do is similar to a man who did not go to school but heard about the graduation ceremony; he runs to the school bookstore to buy the graduation gown and other things. He then proceeds to the hall, well-dressed like one of the real prospective graduates, and makes his way among the students to sit down. He participates in all the activities, such as the singing of the national anthem, the school theme song, all that good stuff.

Quite interestingly, his excitement increases as the others around him are called to the stage to grab their degrees; he was expecting to be called up, too. Yet to his surprise, the last student is called and the folks walked off stage while he remained in his graduation outfit. This guy is so ashamed and embarrassed, especially because he brought friends and family and told them that he was graduating.

That is how many Christians behave when they loosely quote this Bible verse, claiming to reap from where they did not sow. What they miss is that the Philippian church did something that moved the heart of the Apostle Paul before he made such declarations to bless them.

Sadly, many Christians do not do the work that the Philippian church did, but they want the blessings of that hard labor. That is why many people who quote that verse in the wrong way and who expect God to provide continue to be broke, sick and poor – because God will not do a thing until they do what the Philippian church did.

So, what did the Philippians do? Just read below and you will find the simple answer; they gave to the Apostle Paul when he was in great need.

> *15Nevertheless, you have done well that you shared in my distress. 15 Now you Philippians know also that in the beginning of the gospel, when I departed from Macedonia, no church shared with me concerning giving and receiving but you only. 16 For even in Thessalonica you sent aid once and again for my necessities. 17 Not that I seek the gift, but I seek the fruit that abounds to your account. 18 Indeed I have all and abound. I am full, having received from Epaphroditus the things sent from you, a sweet-smelling aroma, an acceptable sacrifice, well pleasing to God. 19 And my God shall supply all your need according to His riches in glory by Christ Jesus.*
> **Philippians 4: 17-19 NKJV**

When you make the wrong declarations without the proper substance of faith and works, you will not receive any answers from God; at least, not what you expect. I bring this up to talk about the power of service. The little Philippians saw a need and filled it. The pastor who preached the gospel to them was in great need. Though they were a small church, they sacrificed all they had to take care of the Apostle Paul and his team, even when he was in Corinth and Thessalonica. The Corinthians and Thessalonians did not cater to him when he was there preaching and teaching the Word of God; they did not support him. It was the little Philippian church that sent constant financial assistance and other supplies. That is why after the Apostle Paul received all the great gifts, he prayed that his God, the God of the heavens and the earth, would supply their needs according to his riches in glory because they took good care of him. So, in simple words, let me say this to you: no service, no rewards; simple as that.

I always knew that serving the clergy has great benefits. I know that fully well because I saw what happened in Gbiso. I grew with my grandmother, the late Ma Phebe D. Nyemah of Gbiso, a powerful woman of God from Maryland in Liberia.

Over the years, as I grew up in Gbiso, for all the people who showed proper honor and gratitude to her, God did great things. The things of God are not just about talking; they are about doing. God wants us to honor him and honor his representatives. God wants us to honor the men and women he has given us as shepherds over us.

The Bible strongly urges us to obey those whom God put over us because they watch over our souls. The pastors and other men and women of God play vital roles in our society. Their prayers and intercessions have great power to save lost souls and minister the grace of God to the saints. Their prayers can do unbelievable things. Like Moses who opened the Red Sea and Joshua who stopped the sun, pastors carry out the work of the Lord. Like Elijah who commanded rain to cease for three and a half years and who caused it to fall again and brought down fire, the Lord uses pastors to do great things.

Like the early disciples whose prayers commanded angels to set pastors free from prisons, or like the worship of Paul and Silas who brought earthquakes in the prison, pastors bring down the glory of God and manifest his power. When pastors take their proper role in society, they affect politics, business and human development. Their work brings lasting change and transformation. Notwithstanding, there are corrupt pastors, but there are also good pastors who do the work of the Lord without compromise. It is because of this that the Bible says we should,

*¹⁶Obey those who rule over you, and be submissive, for they watch out for your souls, as those who must give account. Let them do so with joy and not with grief, for that would be unprofitable for you.* **Hebrews 13:17 NKJV**

If pastors can speak the Word of the Lord in our lives and bring salvation, healing, deliverance, breakthroughs, miracles and encouragement, why would we not honor them by showing proper appreciation to them? They have dedicated their lives to work for God, they fast and pray, struggle with their ministries, and then when God uses them to bless us, we walk away without saying thank you. When we become ungrateful and dishonor them, we dishonor God by not taking proper care of pastors.

The Bible states that we should properly honor the men and women of God. Some of them really deserve double honor – not just any kind of honor, but double honor.

*¹⁷Let the elders who rule well be counted worth of double honor, especially those who labor in the word and doctrine. For the Scripture says, "You shall not muzzle an ox while it treads out the grain," and "The laborer is worthy of his wages."* **I Timothy 5:17-18 NKJV**

Pastors should be compensated, well compensated, but not overly compensated to the extent that all of the church money is going toward the salary of the pastor, vacations and luxuries. While I do not support such extravagant lifestyles of pastors based on church money when their members struggle to find daily bread and live in poor conditions, pastors need to receive appropriate wages for their efforts.

Let me tell you how difficult the lives pastors can be to help you understand why they should receive adequate compensation. I may say a few things here, but it is truly

27

difficult to step in the shoes of real pastors. While the work of pastors is not physical labor, it deals with heavy emotional and spiritual challenges.  Pastors and their families face constant spirit attacks.

Pastors suffer a lot of stress and depression that people do not seem to see.  Quietly, stress from the work of ministry can creep into their lives and even affect their families.  If people do not give this stress proper attention and help their pastors, it leads to depression. Burnout is another serious problem pastors can face.  Pastors work too much; the 60 to 80 hours a week has a way of making them tired if they do not get proper rest to rejuvenate.  It seems that the devil shoots his worst arrows at pastors. Pastors have the same types of problems as any other person: things like work, home affairs, kids, relationships, finances, etc.  Moreover, people criticize pastors quite often; people criticize pastors they do not even know.

Many pastors have sexual problems. Sexual temptation for pastors is at an all-time high because of the nature of their work.  Many people in churches are women.  Women seem to have the most emotional and relationship problems, which is why pastors give council and offer prayers.

Sadly, their empathy and compassion can be easily misconstrued and women can often have feelings for pastors. This mostly comes from women who want husbands and children or have family problems.  There is also a growing trend that women *"fall in love"* with pastors because of the anointing.  They somehow feel that they can get some of the anointing by having sexual relations with the pastors – even though this is far from the truth.

Many pastors who are not that strong can easily find themselves in this mess.  Consequently, the church in the western world, especially the church in America, does not seem to have compassion or *"forgiveness"* for pastors caught in infidelity.  The church usually dismisses pastors like that, and the pastors cannot lead anymore.

Betrayal in the church is a deadly problem. Church members can betray pastors. Disgruntled church leaders can betray pastors. Moreover, the most painful one is when pastors, especially pastors whom other pastors suffer to bring up in the ministry, turn against them and betray them. Though the betrayal of church members is painful and that of church leaders is troublesome, betrayal from pastors within the ministry is deadly. These deceitful pastors can lead members astray, talk bad about their seniors and spread rumors.

Many pastors quit ministry because of the constant betrayal in the church. Betrayal in the church is a deadly disease. It brings out the worst in church members, church leaders and pastors.

Loneliness is another serious problem pastors can face. They have to spend time alone with God in prayer, in planning sermons and reflecting on things. In the wake of these things, loneliness can easily creep in. Many pastors do not have friends. Quite interestingly, pastors are usually advised not to make friends with church members, so many pastors do not have any friends, not even outside the church.

Pastors pray more often, and then fast and pray. Pastors have to be ready, study and pray for their sermons. Pastors work on average 60 to 80 hours a week. The truth is that pastors go through a lot; that is why the Bible teaches us to give them proper honor.

Here are a few things we can do for our pastors or for pastors in general. Let us pray for our pastors. Pastors have a unique call of God upon their lives, but they are not super spiritual beings; they need prayer. We need to pray for our pastors.

Let us protect our pastors against cheap gossip and criticism; this is something we can do to help the church. Do not be the one to spread bad news; rather, protect your pastors. We also need to encourage our pastors greatly. Find your own way to encourage your pastors. They need some affirmation. Help your pastor today; he needs you. In fact, this is what Jesus said about pastors and church leaders. We need to welcome them.

> [18]"*Anyone who welcomes you welcomes me, and anyone who welcomes me welcomes the one who sent me. Whoever welcomes a prophet as a prophet will receive a prophet's reward, and whoever welcomes a righteous person as a righteous person will receive a righteous person's reward.* **Matthew 10:40-41 NIV**

God has given us incentives for honoring his pastors and church leaders. He gives us rewards for our good work. Do not miss yours. To make your pastor remember you always, let your gifts speak for you. I knew it when I was not a pastor and now I know it as pastor. Even though I pray for all my church members regularly, for those who give me gifts as their pastor, I remember them in my prayers always, especially when I think about how they bless my life. I also come to see that the people who properly honor pastors are doing well; sometimes they are even better than other church members are. I want to encourage you to do good to your pastors because it is your duty, but actually, you should do it out of love. Don't forget to measure when you want quick and easy blessings from God; it's then when you really need to give to your pastors. Give because every one of us could use some blessings from God – when you give to your pastors, God blesses your life with rewards.

## b. CHURCH LEADERS

Not all the leaders in the church are pastors; some people play other vital leadership roles. We need to treat pastors and church leaders alike with honor. We cannot say that we respect and honor the pastor but disrespect other church leaders. All of them are doing the work of the Lord and deserve to be honored properly. That is why Jesus put them in various categories, saying that if you receive the disciples, the prophets, the righteous men (the men and women of God) and his other people, you will receive rewards from God.

> *[19]Whoever welcomes a prophet as a prophet will receive a prophet's reward, and whoever welcomes a righteous person as a righteous person will receive a righteous person's reward.* **Matthew 10:41 NIV**

If you receive a righteous man or women because they work for God, you will receive rewards from God. All the children of God have blessings, plenty of blessings attached to their lives; if you want those special blessings, you have to welcome them, honor them, give them money and other gifts – large or small – and treat them well. This is one of the ways God intends to care for his servants; this is so because of all the challenges they go through. It is a win-win situation.

When you give to a pastor or church leader, God gives back to you. I love that. By the way, let me be quick to announce to you that I am a pastor! That means, as one of God's servants, when you receive me, welcome me, promote me, give me gifts and treat me well, God will bless you. Yes, I am right here. God has your rewards; do something so God can release your blessings! Aha, I am joking; oh no, I am dead serious!

## c. SERVING PEOPLE, LAY PEOPLE

It is of great importance for us to serve one another in the Lord. The world today is in need of service, good customer service. Anybody with a good heart and who knows how to talk to people can find life easy. Any business, church or organization that puts service before money always does good. Serving people can be sweet, but it can be hard at times. The truth is, though serving people can be difficult, it is one of the most rewarding things to do. I believe there is joy and fulfillment in serving people, especially people in the church, because God wants us to serve one another. That is why he said that anybody who gives to another, helps another, stands with another, especially those in need, would not lose their reward. You will not lose your reward and I will not lose my reward when we help others.

> *[20]And if anyone gives even a cup of cold water to one of these little ones who is my disciple, truly I tell you, that person will certainly not lose their reward."* **Matthew 10:42 NIV**

When you take good care of God's children, not just for charity, but also for development, God will greatly reward you. That is why those who know that, even for the wrong purposes, still give alms to others – because they are aware of the blessings attached to giving. If this is so, how much more are we to give to others to serve one another out of love?

We need to do more. If you have not been serving people, if you are mean and selfish, you need to change and start to be nice and supportive. Start to give to others and you will be surprised what the Lord will do for you. The truth is that there are lots of Christians and others of God's people who need our help.

What you and I can do will make a great difference somewhere to help others. Do not be like the others who make countless excuses as to why they do not want to help others and serve them. Do not be like that. Be the one whom God can count on to service his people around the world. The Lord is watching us to see what we will do.

## d. EQUALLY REWARDED

I have talked about the need to give to others and serve them because it is the right thing to do. Now I want to talk to you about the nature of the rewards we get in return. God has a way of rewarding everyone based on his own criteria. You and I do not have to privilege to choose our particular reward, but we can be sure that we will get our appropriate rewards. Let me be quick to tell you that sometimes we will not reap the immediate benefits of our hard work, but our families and children can reap the blessings of our hard work.

Jesus told his followers a unique parable that talks about work and service. This story tells us that it really does not matter when we started to work; the master will pay us according to our work here and up in glory. It also teaches us that doing good never ends; there are people with needs everywhere, always. When we do our portion of the work, let us know that we did our part; the Lord will gather others to do their part. Here is the story:

> *21 "For the kingdom of heaven is like a landowner who went out early in the morning to hire laborers for his vineyard. 2 Now when he had agreed with the laborers for a denarius a day, he sent them into his vineyard.3 And he went out about the third hour and saw others standing idle in the marketplace, 4 and said to them, 'You also go into the vineyard, and whatever is right I will give you.' So they went. 5 Again he went out about the sixth and the ninth hour, and did likewise. 6 And about the eleventh hour he went out and found others standing idle,[a] and said to them, 'Why have you been standing here idle all day?' 7 They said to him, 'Because no one hired us.' He said to them, 'You also go into the vineyard, and whatever is right*

*you will receive.'[b] 8 "So when evening had come, the owner of the vineyard said to his steward, 'Call the laborers and give them their wages, beginning with the last to the first.' 9 And when those came who were hired about the eleventh hour, they each received a denarius. 10 But when the first came, they supposed that they would receive more; and they likewise received each a denarius. 11 And when they had received it, they complained against the landowner, 12 saying, 'These last men have worked only one hour, and you made them equal to us who have borne the burden and the heat of the day.' 13 But he answered one of them and said, 'Friend, I am doing you no wrong. Did you not agree with me for a denarius? 14 Take what is yours and go your way. I wish to give to this last man the same as to you. 15 Is it not lawful for me to do what I wish with my own things? Or Is your eye evil because I am good?'*
**Matthew 20:1-15 NKJV**

Your reward will not be like my reward; your work may not be exactly like mine, but we are all working for the Lord to cater to his people. When you and I agree to serve others, we need not compare our rewards with those of others and start to grumble. You may get what you receive from the Lord today; you do not know what the Lord has in store for you. It could even be that our original form of payment is just a bonus and the actual wages are on the way. Let us not rush and charge the Lord with wrongdoing, grumble, complain or say bad words.

*22 But without faith it is impossible to please Him, for he who comes to God must believe that He is, and that He is a rewarder of those who diligently seek Him.*
**Hebrews 11:6 NKJV**

Have faith in God and know that He will give you what you rightly work for, and what you deserve. Learn to wait for God and not rush before you lose your place. Without faith, we cannot please God. We just have to trust Him and believe in Him. Let us understand that God rewards hardworking people with good things. He is a just God. He will give us what we work for; in fact, many times, He gives more because of his grace and favor. I want you to know that God will reward your work.

I hear people complain that they have done good for people and get nothing in return. Many people even say that they are tired of doing good because people are ungrateful. I hear your concern. You may be right, but I think you may be looking too hard or looking in the wrong place. God rewards every good work. Maybe it is true that you did the good work, but your attitude that followed was not good. On the other hand, are you the one doing good just so you can feel good and feel your how important you are, instead of doing it out of love and obedience to God?

I may not know exactly what your problem is, but I will pray for you so that you can reap the benefits of your goodwill. I also know that at times the wicked devil ties down the blessings of people after their hard work just to disprove the word of God in them. He does it to create doubt in you as if God cannot fulfill his word over your life. He wants to make you feel that doing good is not worth it, so you can miss your reward from God. Doing good takes sacrifice. Please stand the test of time. I will be praying for you.

## e.  SERVICE TAKES SACRIFICE

There are so many people who do not really understand how tough it is to serve other people; they do not understand that many times serving people requires sacrifice, personal sacrifice.  They glue their eyes so much on the awards, the recognition and the good name that they overlook the sacrifice.

Let me be quick to say that this does not happen every time we help others call for sacrifice. No, but it is true sometimes; again, let me say that sometimes it takes sacrifice to serve others, even the people of God in the church.

Some of the rudest people on the planet go to church and they take out their rudeness on the ushers, church workers and other leaders. I thank all the ushers who work in various churches for taking all the insults, crossed eyes and rudeness from church members, especially baby mothers!  Many people with troublesome children act as if their kids are so nice and perfect at home when these little kids act like demons destroying things around the house.  Instead of being grateful to the ushers and Children's Church workers, some parents behave rudely.  This is ridiculous!  I almost want to tell them, "Hey, your child is rude just like you!"  Sadly, we cannot say such mean things to people in church; but anyway, God knows our hearts.

This is why I really appreciate all those who work in human services; they do quite excellent work in keeping disgruntled souls under control.  It is not just for the money alone; it is the passion they carry in their hearts to help humanity that compels them to work day after day.  Jesus talked about his death as part of his service to mankind for the redemption of sins.  The deepest service does not sometimes bring the biggest rewards, especially in material goods, but it pays.  Nevertheless, there are times when our most difficult service can yield the best rewards ever!

²³ *Now Jesus, going up to Jerusalem, took the twelve disciples aside on the road and said to them,* ¹⁸ *"Behold, we are going up to Jerusalem, and the Son of Man will be betrayed to the chief priests and to the scribes; and they will condemn Him to death,* ¹⁹ *and deliver Him to the Gentiles to mock and to scourge and to crucify. And the third day He will rise again."* **Matthew 20:17-19 NKJV**

We must be willing to pay the sacrifice it takes to get things done, especially when it comes to serving. When service calls for sacrifice but we are not willing to commit, it makes service useless. Jesus told his disciples and some people that the Son of Man would be betrayed, mocked, scourged, crucified and put to death. He told them that he accepted the sacrifice for his mission and committed to it. Your mission in life comes with a price of sacrifice. I must admit, while the sacrifices vary, it is something serious to deal with. Your price is different from mine. The challenges are real but different. The truth is, they are particular to the person and situation. Whatever the case is, we must be willing to pay the sacrifice for our dreams and visions, for our children and spouses, for our education, for our church, businesses and life itself. Life calls for sacrifice.

## f. SERVICE, NOT PERSONAL GAIN

While it is true that we get rewards from our service to others, it is *not for profit*. Service is about serving humanity from a heart of compassion. Today there are many people who have the heart to help others; they really try hard to help others, even people they do not know. I thank God for all of them. Quite interestingly, there are other people, even well-known people and organizations, that use the plight of the poor and suffering to hoard millions of dollars every year without anyone bringing them to justice. They help only because of the fame, money or some other selfish ambition; they do not do it with good motives. They talk about assisting the poor so much and show sorrowful images of the suffering masses more than the work they actually do; this is not fair at all. Sadly, they collect huge amounts of money and other things from donors around the world in the name of the suffering, yet the suffering does not benefit them much.

Jesus tells us a story of the misplaced ambition of a mother for her children. It makes me think about some parents who will do the stupidest thing to please their children. Their notion of being there for family or friends is warped and misconstrued; they somehow feel that others should honor every silly request. Nevertheless, whatever we want in life for ourselves and our children needs to pass before the morality judge to see if its position and possible impact is all right. Here is the story.

> **24 20** *Then the mother of Zebedee's sons came to Him with her sons, kneeling down and asking something from Him. 21 And He said to her, "What do you wish?" She said to Him, "Grant that these two sons of mine may sit, one on Your right hand and the other on the left, in Your kingdom." 22 But Jesus answered and said, "You do not know what you ask. Are you able to drink the cup that I am about to drink, and be baptized with the baptism that I am baptized with?"[d] They said to Him, "We are able." 23 So He said to them, "You will indeed drink My cup, and be baptized with the baptism that I am baptized with;[e] but to sit on My right hand and on My left is not Mine to give, but it is for those for whom it is prepared by My Father."*
> **Matthew 20: 20-23 NKJV**

The mother wanted her sons who were with Jesus to be glorified more than the others, even though all of them served as one unit. Selfish mama! What a shame that she only sees her two sons and not the twelve disciples, much less the seventy-two. This sort of thinking will always create problems. The mother did not even think about what price was hanging in the balance; she wanted the glory.

She did not know about the betrayal of a close friend, something that really hurts; she wanted the position. She did not think about the flogging, the mockery in the streets, the carrying of the cross, the nails, the spear, the vinegar and the torture to death, even death on the cross with capital sinners; she wanted the power. Oh, how badly we want shortcuts in life!

Her behavior embarrassed her sons among their friends; it stirred up confusion among the others. Some parents seem to like to embarrass their kids in public; that is not good at all.

If we as parents do that, it makes others look down upon us and sometimes insult us. Promotion comes from God, not from man. Let us be mindful of when, where and how we ask for promotion before we disgrace ourselves among important people.

Be careful. Once you serve, there is a reward for you; do not do anything crazy. The one who called to serve sees all things. He knows what time you work hard and what time you play lazy.

He even knows what time you complained, thought about quitting, or looked for something better. God knows it all. He will make others recognize you for your service; do not fight or push your way through prematurely. Your reward is at hand; just wait for the master.

## g. SELFISH AMBITION STIRS UP STRIFE

*25When the ten heard about this, they were indignant with the two brothers. Jesus called them together and said, "You know that the rulers of the Gentiles lord it over them, and their high officials exercise authority over them. Not so with you. Instead, whoever wants to become great among you must be your servant, and whoever wants to be first must be your slave—just as the Son of Man did not come to be served, but to serve, and to give his life as a ransom for many."* **Matthew 20:24-28 NKJV**

In the story stated above, when the other ten disciples heard that the mother of two of their colleagues asked Jesus for special privileges for them, they were angry with the two. Jesus immediately took charge of the situation and taught them a valuable lesson about leadership. Leaders do not fight for positions; people honor them with positions. He told them that they should not be like others who like to be bosses and abuse their power; instead, if they wanted to be leaders, they needed to start to serve. He demonstrated to them that his own life was a ransom for many; he did not come for people to serve him, but he came to serve humanity. As you go about serving others, make sure you are not selfish in your thoughts. Selfishness and service do not go hand in hand. Selfishness is about the individual. Service is about people.

## h. GOOD SERVICE, NOT EYE SERVICE

One valuable lesson I learned from my grandfather was about eye service. This is the type of service people render only for others to see them and know that they are doing something. They want recognition; they do not really seem to have the heart to serve. People like that do not work until they know that someone is looking at them. They do not seem to know that other people are smart enough to know the difference between a diligent worker and a pretender. In their naïve ways, they think they can outsmart everyone without realizing that they have just outsmarted themselves, and shame and dismissal will be their portion. If you want to serve, serve; if you are in it for any selfish reasons, you are in the wrong place. Maybe you should try the *for-profit* sector.

It is because of this that the Apostle Paul told the church in Philippi a powerful message that is good for all of us today, saying:

> *26:12 Therefore, my dear friends, as you have always obeyed—not only in my presence, but now much more in my absence—continue to work out your salvation with fear and trembling, 13 for it is God who works in you to will and to act in order to fulfill his good purpose. 14 Do everything without grumbling or arguing, 15 so that you may become blameless and pure, "children of God without fault in a warped and crooked generation." [c] Then you will shine among them like stars in the sky 16 as you hold firmly to the word of life. And then I will be able to boast on the day of Christ that I did not run or labor in vain.* **Philippians 2: 12-16 NIV**

Be a trusted worker. Be efficient. Do not do it because of the profit you want to get and don't pretend to love something you do not really love; be real for once. We serve God as we serve people. As we serve people, let us do it as unto the Lord; in this manner, no one has to be fictitious. Be real in what you do. There are many smart people, and they know how phony you are whenever you do eye service. If you want to be a good leader, a great leader in the area of service, you have to do it from your heart and then put your mind into it. Remember, there are rewards for everything we do for the Lord, for his pastors, leaders and people. God is watching. Serve with virtue.

Many times I wonder what our world would be like if we really began to serve one another out of love! I think our love would become contagious, and with the advent of the internet and social media, it would become a global phenomenon in no time. Imagine all the players of our sports teams helping one poor neighborhood and challenging their competitors to do the same.

Now imagine that the wealthy people in our cities take on projects in low-income communities and give them a facelift; how wonderful would that be? Imagine if the churches, starting with the rich churches and other religious groups, would begin doing charity in and around their states! How would that be? This thing would spread so quickly that there would not be any beggars and homeless people in the United States of America and around the world.

Think about this: imagine if all the Africans and African-Americans went back to Africa and did some projects all over the continent, with each one picking a country or city in which to invest. Picture a world in which all the Hispanics who are doing well here went back home and began some meaningful projects.

What if every people, group and class were to find a country, a city, a community to invest in; what would our world be over the next few years? It would be quite remarkable! This is the power of service. We can change the world. I can change the world. You can change the world. Together, we can do great things and put our names in the world books of trendsetters!

This is not a farfetched dream. It can become reality only if you and I become the change we want to see and then teach others to do the same. The world today has a lot of selfish rich people. It has so many rich and wicked people. Yet, it also has plenty of good-hearted people who have the heart to serve but no resources. I know how difficult it is to serve without skilled volunteers and resources. I went through that. I want to be quick to tell you: serve even if you do not have quality people and money. Do whatever you can until help comes. I pray that the Lord will make someone or an organization find you and give you all the help you need to serve the people of God in your area. But remember, whether or not you have money and skilled volunteers, serve anyway. Help is on the way!

# Part Three

## PART 3: The LORD Needs It

a. Each One Has Something To Benefit The Other
b. Go Find It
c. Deal With Confrontations
d. Make The Discovery
e. Implementation
f. Declaration
g. Make Your Presentation

# The LORD Needs It

Each one of us has something to give to God. We have something to give to the world to make it a better place for us all. As we go through this chapter, I want you to think about what gifts and abilities or resources you have that you could give to God for service. When we use our gifts and abilities, it gives us pleasure, recognition, money and other opportunities.

Hannah, a barren woman in the Bible, surrendered her miracle son Samuel to Prophet Eli for the service of the Lord after God answered her prayer. Esther used her beauty and brains to give up life to approach the king to plead for her people, her husband, in the place and season where women could not come forth, or face immediate death. A little boy surrendered his lunch to Jesus to feed 5000 people with ten baskets left over. An old poor widow gave her last coin in the offering and Jesus stopped the service to recognize her. So let me ask you, how can that talent, ability, idea or strength you have be used to glorify God and help humanity?

Apart from the Bible, there are people in society who have used their talents and abilities to give the world something valuable, something to help make it a better place in which to live. Somebody discovered electricity, the Wright brothers gave the world airplanes, Bill Gates gave us Microsoft, Mark Zuckerberg gave us Facebook, Steve Jobs gave us the iPhone and Apple products, etc. In the different disciplines of life, there are people who invented things or improved on things that really made a difference. Again, let me ask you, what do you have that God could bless, magnify and spread to help others? What do you have to give?

JAMES C. NYEMAH

## a. EACH HAS SOMETHING TO BENEFIT THE OTHER

Each one of us has something that the Lord needs. It is something that, when given, the Lord can use, bless, multiply and make a blessing on us, our families and the world. Using our gifts and abilities will put us in high places.

*27A man's gift makes room for him, and brings him before great men.* **Proverbs 18:16 NKJV**

Your gift will create a platform for you. It will make room for you to show your worth. Your gift will bring you before great men and women to make your voice known. Your gift will speak for you, even in your absence. There is something very important about the natural and spiritual endowments the Lord has given each one of us. God intends for you to prosper because of your gift. Money, work, space, things – all connect to your gift. When you have these things and more, you will begin to live a different and better life. There are some people I did not know, but accepting the call of the Lord for ministry has connected me to many precious people I would never have met.

When we use our gifts, they bring us notoriety, fame, money, people and things. Our gifts will take us places, high places. Your gift, talent and ability can give you your own platform on which to operate rather than fighting over space that belongs to others. By the way, why would you fight over another person's platform when you can create a better one in a great location? There is no need for that; all we need to do is to begin to use all the talents, gifts and abilities the Lord gave us.

Sadly, there are many people who have resources, gifts, talents and abilities that they are not using. Many of them will carry these things to their graves. They make the graveyard a barnyard for untapped potential. What a travesty! It would have been better for them to collaborate with others and do something. It would have been better if they had started something, taught others how to manage it and moved on to other things rather than let the precious gift die with them. They do not give it to others, nor do they give it to the Lord to use. To everybody's loss, they keep what we are looking for. This is one of humanity's worst predicaments – wasted gifts!

In preparation for the week of the passion of the Christ, Jesus told his disciples to go ahead and bring a donkey so that he could use it, though it was not for them. In the story that follows, Jesus, the disciples and the owner of the donkey all worked in unison to bring us a touching story of service and passion. Let me take you through it step by step. I want you to remember that we are talking about things, talents, gifts and abilities we possess that could be used for the service of the Lord. Follow me.

*28 "Go to the village ahead of you, and as you enter it, you will find a colt tied there, which no one has ever ridden. Untie it and bring it here. 31 If anyone asks you, 'Why are you untying it?' say, 'The Lord needs it.'"32 Those who were sent ahead went and found it just as he had told them. 33 As they were untying the colt, its owners asked them, "Why are you untying the colt?" 34 They replied, "The Lord needs it."35 They brought it to Jesus, threw their cloaks on the colt and put Jesus on it.* **Luke 19:30-35 NIV**

I love this story. It is simple and short, but powerful. There are a few things I want to bring up for our discussion. These things will help us understand our discussion better. It shows us how our obedience to use our gifts, talents and abilities can serve a greater purpose. Even though they will satisfy their immediate purpose, there is something bigger we need to consider as well. Let me break it down in a few steps.

47

## b. GO FIND IT.

Jesus told the disciples to go ahead in the city where they would find a young donkey; they needed to untie it and bring it back for him to use. This is what the Bible says:

*[29] "Go to the village ahead of you, and as you enter it, you will find a colt tied there, which no one has ever ridden. Untie it and bring it here.* **Luke 19:30 NKJV**

We have a few things we need to work on. Here is the breakdown. In verse 30 we have a command to *"Go, Enter there, Find it"*, yes, find that valuable thing or person and bring it to the Lord for service.

We need to *"Go, Enter, Find, Bring"* our total selves to service of the Lord. God wants to use every part of us for his glory. Whatever natural and spiritual endowments, talents, gifts and abilities we have, we need to surrender them to him. Besides what we have within us, there is a world out there to discover.

There are others, perhaps others around us, nearby in our families and communities, who, too, have something wonderful to give. We need to go out there, enter the place, find them and bring them to the Lord. There are others out there who may not look like us.

Whether they have different backgrounds and different social and economic statuses, all of them need to come as well. Let us *"Go, Enter, Find and Bring"* anyone and anything the Lord can use. Remember, just one word or one touch from the Lord is sufficient to change anybody or anything.

## c. DEAL WITH CONFRONTATIONS

We must learn the art of handling confrontations, not running from them or complaining all day long.

*[30] "If anyone asks you, 'Why are you untying it?' you shall say, 'The Lord has need of it."* **Luke 19:31 NKJV**

In verse 31 we are commanded to know how to deal with the people and things that confront us as we carry out the Lord's command to *Go, Enter, Find, Bring.* We must plainly tell them that *"The Lord needs it."* Our second step is to know how to deal with confrontations, not run from them or complain all day long. Every day a battle rages in and around us. It is a battle we can win. This battle challenges us as to whether we can take charge of our lives and do something better or let circumstances dictate our responses. There are people, things, places and spirits that confront us even when we are trying to do something good. In fact, it appears that even sometimes when we stay out of other people's business, problems still arise to confront us. So, technically speaking, it is not about doing something or not doing it, but the mere fact that we exist. Now let me ask you, should you and I cease to exist because situations confront us? My answer is a big no. Wherever we go, wherever we turn, it is easy to find opposition.

Jesus taught the disciples how to deal with the confrontations ahead of the mission. I think we need to do the same as well. We all have missions we need to fulfill. Let us learn a few things from this story. This reminds me of a story: when the Lord called me to ministry in Tabou, Ivory Coast. The Lord spoke to me to gather a team to sing and do ministry. One of the girls asked me how sure I was that the Lord wanted her to be a part of my team and why

God never spoke to her. I had to find an answer to this. I quickly prayed in my heart and asked the Lord to help me. I simply told her to ask the Lord if it was he who told me to talk with her about becoming part of the team if she was not sure. That settled the problem. When I gave her the answer, the Lord spoke to my heart; it answered her, calmed her down and convinced her to be a part of the team. All we really need to do is ask the Lord what to do with confrontations if he did not tell us in the beginning.

*[31] "If anyone asks you, 'Why are you untying it?' you shall say, 'The Lord has need of it.'"* **Luke 19:31 NIV**

All the disciples needed to handle the confrontation was to tell the people that the Lord had need of it. When you and I go out there to call people to join us to serve the Lord or to tell them to use their talents and abilities and they ask troubling questions, we can tell them that the Lord needs them.

Speaking the word of the Lord in the confrontation will let them know that we are not alone. It tells them that there is a bigger and greater force behind us. It tells us that we are the messengers and that we do not need to act like the boss unless he gives us the exclusive right to do so. It is not the number of words that count here, but the power that lies in simple, spoken words that have virtue. It is speaking the word of the Lord to anyone who dares to ask.

Let me bring this home and make it personal. Whenever you try to develop, implement or shine in your gifts and talents, you will have opposition. Opposition comes from internal and external forces – places, things, spirits or people whom you do not know who oppose your success. Internal forces have two parts.

The first part is from people close to you; it could be your friends and family. The second and most difficult part is within yourself. It happens when you have fear and insecurity. It happens when you are emotionally, mentally and spiritually unfit to handle your own success.

There are always people who seemingly come from nowhere to attack. It is sometimes so sickening to see that not all the people who confront or oppose us are total strangers. Most of them are actually friends and family. They seem to not believe in you but are quick to condemn things they do not understand. Instead of asking, encouraging or even supporting you, they are ready to break you down.

## d. MAKE THE DISCOVERY

The third step is to discover that things are the way they should be. One good thing to know in working on a project is that all the resources are available and in the right place. It is quite relieving. When the disciples went on to the town ahead of them, they saw the young donkey tied to a tree, just as Jesus told them. Their work was easy. The saw the prize; all they needed now was to deal any unfriendly fire and move on. For them, it was a great experience. They saw the donkey and the owners. Let me be quick to say that not everything the Lords sends us to find is easily accessible. Some things are like gold, hidden in the earth. We have to get muddy before we can find them. Sometimes we have to fight hard before we can spot our trophy. I want you to know that things are not always easy. I thank God that our fellow disciples found the donkey as the Lord has said.

*[32]So those who were sent went away and found it just as He had told them.* **Luke 19:32 NIV**

In verse 32 we see that things will be the way the Lord told us they would be as we *Go, Enter, Find, Bring*. It is a sad thing that many people do not go where the Lord has sent them, thereby not seeing things the way they should be.

Some people add to what the Lord has told them and make their own missions to satisfy their egos instead of following orders from above. When you are in the right place, where the Lord wants you to be, things will be the way God said they would be.

There are many people who think somehow that if there is difficulty in your journey, you are not in the will of God. Some would say to pastors in ministry that the anointing of God has lifted upon them, given them the perfect opportunity to break away. That is not true.

I am here to dispute that. Jesus told the disciples to expect opposition and gave them instructions on how to handle it. Therefore, when you experience opposition in your life, in your business, in your ministry or family, it does not necessarily mean that the Lord is not with you. Opposition is something we should handle; when we do, we will enjoy the miracle of overcoming it. Jesus told the disciples that there would be opposition, but showed them how to handle it. I declare the word of the Lord unto you today, that you will have power and everything it takes to overcome every opposition in your life in the name of Jesus. You will see things the way God said. It does not matter or not whether you face trouble because the God of miracles is your God. God will help you overcome every obstacle in the mighty name of Jesus. You will discover that things are the way the Lord said they will be.

## e. IMPLEMENTATION

The fourth step is to implement the instructions of the Lord, not change them or compromise. Knowing to do something is good, and seeing that things are the way they should be is even better, but regardless of how things might be, if we do not implement them properly, it is a waste of time. Manifestation of our gifts and abilities is of vital importance.

Imagine that you went to your favorite restaurant with your special someone to dine and you talked so much about how nice the place is, but to your surprise when the waiters bring the food, it is not cooked well; as a matter of fact, the waiter uses her bare hands to try to fix the mess. Although you are ready to dine and relax and it is your favorite restaurant, I do not think you should eat food that is not properly cooked. It does not matter whether the food is usually delicious; when the preparation is bad and even nasty, safety comes to mind right away. You will not eat the food.

If your favorite team played slowly and weakly and missed goals, you would not be happy, especially after paying to attend its practice games. Knowing how well they did in practice, you would be totally disappointed to see them lose after you bought an expensive ticket to sit in a good seat just to see them play. Why am I bringing all these things to you? It is a matter of implementation; it is a matter of doing what we are supposed to do. When we go on the business of the Lord, God expects us to carry out his commands accurately. You and I must remember that for every assignment, lives of people, God's people, are at stake.

If you fail in implementation, other people could be hurt or miss their miracles. When we fail in implementation, we lose the lesson to learn and the experience to gain; we rob God of the glory to make his name great in the situation. Understanding this will help you and me take the call of God seriously.

It should make us take time with the commands of God. When we do things correctly, God does the miracle we expect or the miracle beyond our wildest imagination. I challenge you today to implement the commands of the Lord properly. The verse below talks about implementation and confrontation. This is what the Bible says:

> [33]*As they were untying the colt, its owners said to them, "Why are you untying the colt?"* **Luke 19:33 NIV**

In verse 33 we experience confrontations as we *"Go, Enter, Find, Bring."* It is a travesty that many people run away or quit their calling, work, education or business because other people and things challenge them instead of dealing the situation as instructed. We should never quit because of any opposition we experience as we carry out the commands of the Lord. The word God gives us has power; all we need to do is say the word to those who confront us. When we do that, it will settle the case. We have to trust God.

## f. DECLARATION

The fifth step is to say the Word from the Lord. So many people have a powerful word from the Lord that will make a difference, but they never say the word. They somehow think that it is about them and their personal power. At times, they look at their own humanity and struggles and somehow feel inadequate to speak the word of the Lord. In their insecurity, they feel that the word will not work. Moreover, because of this, they do not speak the word of the Lord. They do not want to speak the word of the Lord, especially if that word belongs to some senior people. They forget that the word of the Lord has power of its own. The word of God does not need your help and it does not need my help. You and I need the word of the Lord in our lives today.

Let us learn from the disciples and speak as the Lord commands. It does not matter to whom the word goes; all we need is to say the word. I learned this valuable lesson early on in the ministry, that I need to speak the word and not think otherwise. All we need to do is declare the word of the Lord; this word has its own power. I doubted my own ability and it caused me to doubt the power of God without realizing it. This mistake caused me more trouble. Please do not be like me; just do what the Lord commands you.

*34They said, "The Lord has need of it."* **Luke 19:34 NIV**

In verse 34 when we experience confrontations as we *Go, Enter, Find, Bring,* we must simply speak the Word to the people, things and spirits that confront us. When we do, they will listen because there is power in the word. We need to believe the power of the word of God. We can trust this power. We can rely on it. We can count on it. We can use it with great confidence. I encourage you today to declare the word of God wherever you are and to whomever the Lord sends you. Declare the word.

There are many people today, especially so-called pastors, prophets, apostles and bishops, who do not believe in the power of the word of God; they add other things to make it work. They seem to believe that there is no power in the word of God. Because of this, they go on joining secret societies for power. Others do voodoo because they want power. I want you to know that not every pastor, prayer mother, holy father, prophet, apostle or bishop is from God. Many of them are mediums of evil representation. They carry strange spirits. They make unusual sacrifices. They pay tribute to other gods out there. They go here and there to buy power without thinking about the lives at stake. Quite interestingly, these sorts of pastors are doing very well in our communities because many people want miracles and do not care if the pastor or prayer mother is real, fake or dangerous. All they want is the miracle.

While these so-called pastors and prayer mothers are very wrong, I want to share the blame with the church members and people in our communities who go to them. Many people do not like the pastor who preaches and teaches the uncompromised word of God.

They do not like pastors who preach about sin, repentance, holiness or the judgment of God. When pastors preach these messages, church members sometimes withhold their money for tithes and offerings because they do not like to hear anything like that. This is what gives rise to many pastors seeking other mediums for power to perform miracles: so members will give money.

Church members and other attendants want to pay for miracles, but many of them do not seem to care about knowing God for themselves. They want miracles, but they do not want the God of the miracles. They want miracles, but they do not want to follow any requirement for a blessed life of continuous miracles.

All they want is miracles; because of this, they prefer going to pastors and prayer mothers who can perform miracles. After all, for them it is only about miracles and not a desire to know God and have a genuine relationship with him.

Regardless of the manipulations of people, churchgoers or pastors, God expects us to declare his word without remorse or compromise. In addition, when we do, great things will happen. I want to encourage all the great people out there who are obeying the call of God: when things are difficult, do not give up; we serve the God of miracles. He will bring to pass in your life what he said in his word. I believe for you. Believe.

## g. MAKE YOUR PRESENTATION

The sixth step is to carry the trophy back to the Lord for service. All of us must give account of what the Lord has commanded us to do. We must give account of all the people, things and places we encounter. It is my ardent hope that when your day comes to make your presentation before the Lord, you will have something good to offer. There is something good you need to know. For some people, this presentation is a test of character. For others, it is for your promotion. I pray for you that when your time comes to show God what you have done with his mission, you will have something good to show.

Sometimes, our mission is part of a greater mission; it is not the end. The mission of the disciples was to bring the young donkey. They fulfilled their mission. Upon presenting the donkey, they saw that Jesus began to use the donkey for a greater purpose. Think for a moment: if the disciples failed in their mission, how would Jesus have fulfilled an old Scripture about the Messiah riding on a young donkey to enter into the city of Jerusalem?

I do not know what mission you have and how that relates to other, greater missions, but one thing I want to tell you is that you need to work hard to fulfill your mission. Some things are on a need-to-know basis; that means you may not know what happens next. Regardless of what type of mission you and I have, what is important is for us to fulfill our missions. The disciples fulfilled their mission, and Jesus began his mission. Their obedience to God and fulfillment of their mission initiated the passion of the Christ. This is what the Bible says:

*35They brought it to Jesus, and they threw their coats on the colt and put Jesus on it.* **Luke 19:35 NIV**

It is funny that some people feel their mission is more important than that of others when all of us are working for the Lord. Every mission is an important mission. We need to place great value on every mission because we do not know what the Lord will make out of our obedience. We do not know if our mission will initiate a great vision or bless the lives of others, especially people who could not receive anything otherwise. I respect every missionary. Whether you work in the home, marketplace, church or anywhere else, your mission is important. Fulfill it with passion.

Do you ever wonder why tickets have seat numbers for airplanes, theaters and stadiums? Aha, now you are thinking about how important the work of ushers is. They may not be the bosses, but when they do not do their work, there will be a total mess because people will be fighting over seats. I mention this to say that every mission and every missionary is important. I challenge you to focus on your mission and fulfill it. We may never understand the value until we get to a higher ground and see beyond the horizon.

In verse 35 we experience joy in seeing our portion of the ministry, mission or job completed when we *Go, Enter, Find, and Bring*. When we do our part, the Lord begins to fulfill the purpose of our calling. It is so strange these days that many people are taking credit for things they did not do. Would it not be embarrassing if the actual person who did the work shows up while the one who did not work is bragging and toting the trophy around on stage? I bet it would be! Do not try to be like other people; be yourself. Do not envy others because of their missions; focus on yours. When we work hard to fulfill our mission in life, we will experience the joy of completion. This, I tell you, is quite remarkable.

Some people worry about what others will say about their mission. Sadly, they miss the mark. When you focus on your mission and working hard to fulfill it, you will not have time to look over your shoulders to see what others are doing. It is very important that we focus on the mission and not worry about the noises around us. Do not worry about the critics; that is what critics do best. They criticize people. Give them a chance to do their work, and you go on and do what the Lord has commanded you to do. Do not worry about what about anyone says or does; focus on your mission.

There are many people out there, but the Lord found you worthy and picked you for the mission. Do not ask me why the Lord picked you for the mission, but one thing I can tell you is that fulfilling the mission gives you a certain joy. In fact, your mission adds value to the purpose of your life. It increases your worth in the eyes of people. You should be grateful that you have something to do, unlike many other people wandering the streets looking for what they did not lose. I encourage you to take your mission seriously. There are rewards in its fulfillment.

Whatever people say is not your business; if they have any problems, tell them to talk to the one who sent you. Tell all the moaners, the complainers, the critics and every other person who bothers you to go see God. Send them to see God and go about your business to fulfill your mission. There is no time to play or mess around. Do not let any loser make you miss the mark. Do not let the haters delay you. In fact, you do not owe them any answer; but if you must answer, just send them to talk to God. Thank you.

# Part Four

## PART 4: I AM PREGNANT

a. You Have Proper Endowment
b. Pregnant With a Vision
c. Troubled Because of the Pregnancy
d. Pray For Your Pregnancy
e. The Pregnancy is Personal
f. Sacrifice for the Pregnancy

# I am Pregnant

I am pregnant. Moreover, I must say this to you: you are pregnant, too. I guess I should say that we are pregnant; yes, we all are pregnant. It is not a pregnancy as in the biology of women; no, it is about vision driven by purpose. This pregnancy has great potential. I am pregnant with a vision that has so much potential to change everything and everyone that comes closer. It is a pregnancy that changes the lives of people, transforms communities and develops nations. This pregnancy makes room for gifts and talents hidden within people and unearths them for deployment to benefit the world. There are people who depend on your pregnancy to share the expectancy, share the joy, enjoy the company, and benefit for being connected and empowered to do likewise. Join me as I discuss the issue of pregnancy.

## a. YOU HAVE PROPER ENDOWMENT

God has given each of us a particular deposit in our spirits to do something meaningful and become the best in our class. You have a special endowment and I have mine as well. Some people seem to have multiple talents and gifts while others seem to have only one they can master. Whether you have a single gift, or multiple gifts and talents, what matters the most is the proper deployment to bring about lasting change in the world.

God is not gender-biased or racist as some people are; what he gives to men, he gives to women in wisdom and ingenuity. Whatever God gives to black people, he gives to white and brown people and every race in between. All of us have special talents and gifts that we need to use properly. All of us have what it takes to make the word a better place for ourselves and our children, and generations to come. You have what it takes to overcome adversity and do greater works.

*[36] You, dear children, are from God and have overcome them, because the one who is in you is greater than the one who is in the world.* **I John 4:4 NIV**

In an unapologetic manner, the Scriptures say that there is someone greater on the inside of us; that means all of us, no matter our race, color, ethnicity, social or economic status. We all have the same thing. For some reason, in times past other people felt that they were better than some and treated them worse than brute animals. In fact, some people still believe that their race is better than others are, but that is not true. The sad truth is that if we all had equal opportunities put in the same place; we would all do something to move forward. In addition, sometimes the people who think their race is better than those of others would be surprised that the others can do better than they can. I mention this to say that whatever the Lord does, he does it indiscriminately, for he is a just God.

Most of the appearances of one people or race being better than others is a matter of equal opportunity and fairness. If all groups became modern and developed without interruption from thieves, tyrants and terrorists, things would be so different today. I am left to wonder, what if Africa had not been conquered and driven into slavery on white plantations in America and Europe? What would our world leadership look like today? Who would be leading in technology, science, medicine and human development and innovation?

There are those who selfishly work hard to create limitations for others while pushing others forward. While racism, slavery and discrimination were outlawed, sadly, they are practiced at high levels in many civil societies today. This is manifested in education, employment, politics, business and even in religion.

I want to tell you that we all have something good inside of us. You have something good inside you. I have something. All the other people out there have something good to give society, but many people do not use their gifts. When people do this, they create a vacuum in leadership and many other disciplines in life. I see that many young people go around like vagabonds and half-educated fools. It should not be so because everyone has something wonderful to contribute to our human development.

I see many miserable old folks who have lived their lives and who are now in regret because they have not done anything better. When time and opportunity came knocking, they abused it. Now when their bodies start to fail and time is far spent, a few of them want to do something. They wish they had more time, but all they can do now is whatever they can with whatever time that is left for them.

Time affects our vision; it affects our pregnancy. Time can grow and nurture our pregnancy and vision, and time can cause miscarriage or abortion. Be careful, be very careful with your natural and spiritual endowments, because they are the essence of your life. Your purpose, passion, happiness, friends, connections, fame, finance and notoriety depend on what the Lord put inside of you. Be care with your vision because there are others who like to steal stuff that does not belong to them. Be careful because there are pretenders and imitators who want to mirror your affairs and make a quick profit out of you. Be careful because there are kidnappers out there. They could steal you and everything you live for. Be very careful.

## b. PREGNANT WITH A VISION

I want to discuss a few people whom we can emulate as we discuss the topic of being pregnant with a vision. The first candidate is the Apostle Paul. From the day he had the Macedonia call, his life was never the same. Though he was already working for the Lord, something happened when he responded to that particular call. I mention this to say that no matter what you are doing, when God speaks to your heart a certain thing to do, you need to respond to him. Only God knows the place where our gifts, talents, abilities, goods and services are needed the most. He knows where we would make the most impact, the most profit, and be equally rewarded. We should never be stagnant and not move; whenever God says it is time to go, we must yield to him and move on, no matter what we are doing.

I wonder what one single vision can do to your life and everyone else connected to you and the world at large. How can your vision change the world? This is what the Bible says about the Apostle Paul:

> [37]*Now when they had gone through Phrygia and the region of Galatia, they were forbidden by the Holy Spirit to preach the word in Asia. After they had come to Mysia, they tried to go into Bithynia, but the Spirit did not permit them. So passing by Mysia, they came down to Troas. And a vision appeared to Paul in the night. A man of Macedonia stood and pleaded with him, saying, "Come over to Macedonia and help us." Now after he had seen the vision, immediately we sought to go to Macedonia, concluding that the Lord had called us to preach the gospel to them.* **Acts 16:6-10 (NKJV)**

There are a few things I want to point out here about being pregnant with vision. It is about listening to God and obeying his leadership. The Apostle Paul was on an evangelistic tour. Quite interestingly, the Holy Spirit told him not to preach the word of God in Asia. Wait a minute; that is conflicting with the Great Commission that tells us to go out into the world and preach to everyone. This is it.

> [38]*Then Jesus came to them and said, "All authority in heaven and on earth has been given to me. Therefore, go and make disciples of all nations, baptizing them in the name of the Father and of the Son and of the Holy Spirit, and teaching them to obey everything I have commanded you. And surely I am with you always, to the very end of the age."* **Matthew 28:18-20 NIV**

Inasmuch as the Lord Jesus himself commands us to go out and preach the gospel, he knows better than you and me in any situation and expects us to listen to him and follow his new orders. Because God is omnipotent and omniscient, we ought to listen to him and obey him in any situation even if it seems to be in conflict with other commands. Though it was right for the Apostle Paul to preach anywhere, including Phrygian and Galatia, it was much better for him to listen to the leading of the Holy Spirit because his entire ministry rested upon his obedience to the Lord. Plenty of people in leadership today are not pliable; they are not teachable or expandable. The Lord looks above the horizon, looks beyond the bird's-eye view and can see the big picture. If God wants us to settle a call within a call, why not answer yes and do more than try to tell God what we want to do, as well as when, where and how to do it when we can simply obey him and experience the adventure of a lifetime?

Two times the Apostle Paul tried to enter regions and cities to preach, but the Spirit forbade him to go. However, when he and his team got to Troas, a place destined for change, the Lord spoke to him in a vision. I want to be quick in saying that many times people miss the mark because they are in the wrong place to experience the call of God or the miracle of God. The Apostle Paul needed to be in the right place to hear from God in a unique way. It is not that God did not want the people in those other places to be saved or to be blessed by the ministry; no, not so. However, the Apostle Paul needed to attend to a more urgent call made to God by some desperate people in Macedonia; some people got on their knees to pray and God heard their prayers. There are special needs and emergencies to which heaven must respond. God wants to elevate you and make you one of his Special Forces!

Others might do normal ministry, but God has something better for you to do and that has some special grace and reward attached to it beyond your usual scope. If you say yes to God to make you expandable so that you can take care of his special operations, your life, family, address, finances, travel, connections and even the places you eat will change. When you take the special assignments of God, though they may have high risk, the grace of God that covers you will become different. When you accept the call of God to put out that invention, bring forth those goods and services, heaven is ready to lift you on a completely new level. This is not limited to church work. It applies to every area of life, every business, every project, whether big or small. Sometimes you and I become the first people God contacts to fulfill his mission. Are we going to fail God and let him call on others to do our work while we roam the streets doing nothing interesting? Or are we going to jump on board and *Do the Greater*?

This was more than a typical communication for the Apostle Paul; it was a call to preach to a special group of people he was not thinking about at the time. For me, I say to God, please interrupt my day anytime, anywhere; I want to be on your special team for remarkable assignments. It does not matter what I do and who is benefitting at the moment; whenever heaven calls, I want to answer that call. I know deep down within my heart that if God wants to move me to do something else, he is going to raise up other people to take my place or provide partners I can supervise to do the work I was doing. He is only adding to my team and lifting me higher. I pray today, oh God, that you will bring me new team members to work with so that when the time comes for your special assignment, I can jump in line to fulfill it without question. Regardless of however it comes, please prepare me for the job at hand. My brothers and sisters, all of us need to have such thinking. Let God have his way in your life and you will have more meaning.

We need to learn a good lesson here from the Apostle Paul. God wanted to get him to a place wherein he could be rightly tuned into him to receive his special assignment. However, this was not part of Paul's original mission trip; the Lord created the conditions that necessitated the vision. We have to let God work his miracle in us so that he can give us or activate something greater on the inside of us. God wants us to *"Do the Greater."* God wants to use our passion, our personalities and everything within us to bring about his perfect plan for humanity.

There are some people with good gifts and talents, but they never stop for a moment to let that resonate in them. I must tell you that your vision can create room for personal growth and development. Your gifts, talents and abilities, coupled with your passion, usually power your vision. Your vision, your gift, your talent can take you in front of leaders and royalty, so it is important that we all give it proper attention.

A lot of great people around the world today who shared the story behind their vision and how it began can tell us of the time they had to spend thinking things through before sharing their vision with others. They had to be in a certain place and a certain frame of mind for them to give birth to such great innovations. It is an amazing experience.

Do you have ideas in your head about something wonderful that is not too clear? You are not alone. You need to spend some time alone, reflect on them, and ask the Lord to speak to you. I believe that when you clear your mind of unnecessary things, the Lord will direct you and speak to you. You could be the one to give birth to a new thing that will help people, make money or push you forward in life.

We disappoint God, rob ourselves, cheat our families, friends and the world when we do not let that God-given vision come alive in us because we are so busy doing nothing, acting like we do not care or simply doing useless things. Many times I wonder what would have happened if people like Dr. Martin Luther King, Jr. (who cleared the way to end discrimination against Blacks and other minorities), Bill Gates (who gave us computers and Microsoft software), Steve Jobs (who gave us the Apple computer and the iPhone), Mark Zuckerberg (who gave us Facebook), Nelson Mandela (who created peace in South Africa) or other great people did not let their vision come to light; what our world be today? What if there were no Google, Bing or Wikipedia? What would things look like today? I know some of you cannot imagine living without these things today.

These people had an idea, a vision, a certain pregnancy and gave rise to something powerful that changed the world and made a great impact. Today the world knows them quite well. They make millions and billions of dollars, have notoriety and we love them. Other great people around the world do great things. We love them because they help make our world a better place for everyone. Now, let me ask you a few simple questions. What do we know you for? Where is your name written? Who is talking about you? How important are you to society besides just living and working to survive?

Vision is a powerful thing. It changes one from being a *"nobody"* to becoming a *"somebody."* The Macedonian call changed the Apostle Paul's life. It added value. Today God is still looking for people to impregnate with special visions that will change the world. Paul did it; so did Nelson Mandela, Bill Gates, Mark Zuckerberg, Steve Jobs and many other people around the world. So what about you? What are you doing about your vision? Are you sleeping at the wrong time, playing lazy or just refusing and running from your call?

If you are running from your vision because it looks too big and makes you scared, you are not alone. Most visions are not child's play; they are huge obstacles to overcome and bring lasting change. You are not alone. The truth is, your vision is supposed to be bigger than you are, especially if it is going to be something that touches others around the world. We have small dreams to do this and become that, but there is something greater the Lord has put inside of us.

My vision is bigger than I am; it is bigger. I mean very big. In fact, some part of the vision is a vision within a vision; I call it *"a call within a call."* It really gets my attention. There are times when I am very concerned about my vision. It is not that I do not believe that God will bring it to pass, but I am just uneasy until I can see it in reality.

A few years ago, the Lord gave me a vision to my country, Liberia, to conduct leadership conferences across the nation. I did not know how to do it and did not have the money or partners, but I took it to the Lord in prayer. When I accepted the call, I prayed about it and the Lord helped me find partners; we got the money and manpower required. We made a couple of trips conducting leadership conferences across Liberia. If God did it for me, I am sure that he will do more for you, if only you believe.

## c. TROUBLED BECAUSE OF THE PREGNANCY

The vision the Lord gives has a way to overwhelm. It speaks to the joining of our soul and spirit, bones and marrow, and takes a toll on our mortal bodies. The calling of the Lord in any area of life can be heavy and burdensome and keep people awake, even in the middle of the night when others are sleeping. When it is time for the special thing to happen, our souls can know no rest until things are fulfilled in us. The same was true for Jesus on the night Judas betrayed him. Here is the account.

> *39Then Jesus came with them to a place called Gethsemane, and said to the disciples, "Sit here while I go and pray over there." And He took with Him Peter and the two sons of Zebedee, and He began to be sorrowful and deeply distressed. Then He said to them, "My soul is exceedingly sorrowful, even to death. Stay here and watch with Me."* **Matthew 26:36-38 NKJV**

At the end of his regular activities of ministry, Jesus ate the last supper with the disciples, after which he went to their usual place to pray. Though this was not his first time there, this time, it was special. This would be the last time he went there until he fulfilled his earthly ministry. It would be the place where the Son of Man was delivered into the hands of men, the ruthless Roman army at midnight, for serious beatings after a midnight interrogation without any representation. Jesus knew all this, but the disciples did not have a clue. They thought it was their regular prayer time, but this would be a violent test of faith, a place where Peter would put out his sword to cut a man's ear and the other disciples would get arrested. It was a tough situation ahead.

During our time of overwhelming trouble due to birthing our vision or implementing it, it might not always be easy, so we need to get ready. One night changed the story of Jesus and the disciples. If he was to be the savior of the world, the path to tread would be enduring the court's judgment, beating, agony and death. When our vision is coming alive or going to another level, it causes friction and tension. It takes sacrifice. It takes serious commitment. It is not a joking matter.

It is a matter of life and death for many people, some of whom we may not know. This is a serious thing that heaven can entrust only to strong and committed people. This is not for jokers. This is not for quitters. This is for serious-minded people. Are you ready?

## d. PRAY FOR YOUR PREGNANCY

You must pray for your pregnancy. Pray for your vision. Pray for your dream to come true. A lot of people have a special calling from the Lord to do different things, things that will benefit them, establish them and give them notoriety; sadly, they get busy working on things, but do not take the time to pray for their vision. They forget that there is a thief who steals, kills and destroys anything he can find. Do not let it be you! This is what Jesus said about the enemy and his operations; pay attention to this carefully.

*[40]The thief comes only to steal and kill and destroy; I have come that they may have life, and have it to the full.*
**John 10:10 NIV**

The thief is lurking around, looking for weak links, vulnerable men and women who act carelessly with their God-given vision. They forget that the enemy does not want anything to happen to them. They ignore the fact that their gift, talent, product or service can make our world a better place and help others. They overlook the reality that sometimes it is just one idea, one invention, one gift, talent or ability that can push people forward in life.

While some people have many gifts and talents, others need just one to make it in life. Now, let me ask you an honest question, just a simple one. How many gifts or talents do you have and what are you doing for your society? The Apostle Paul used his gift and ministry to change the world outside of Israel. Nelson Mandela touched the world with peace and a gentle spirit. Bill Gates gave us Microsoft, computers, etc. Steve Jobs gave us the Apple computer and the iPhone. Mark Zuckerberg gave us Facebook. Billy Graham gave us evangelism and mission work. Now, you tell me: where should we put your name and what should we say about it?

Your vision can happen only when you work on it tirelessly and pray for it. Even if things are not working out at the moment, you need to press on, work hard and pray for it to come to pass.

*[41]Then the Lord answered me and said; "Write the vision and make it plain on tablets, that he may run who reads it. For the vision is yet for an appointed time; but at the end it will speak, and will not lie. Though it tarries, wait for it; because it will surely come, it will not tarry."* **Habakkuk 2:2-3 NKJV**

When things get tough while working on your vision, it is time to pray. When critics are climbing on your back and confronting you on every side, it is time to pray. When you do not know how to move on and think about quitting, you really need to pray. When you do not have partners to help you achieve your goals for the vision, my friend, you have to pray. When there is a sort of peace but you have some premonitions and uncertainty, do not let the temporary calm fool you; get up and pray.

There are times when things do not work out the way we planned them; when those times come, we need to be smart and call on God for intervention. God spoke his word through the Prophet Habakkuk that we need to expose the vision; we need to write it down on tablets, on websites, blogs, newspapers or social networks and wherever possible. When the proper time comes to expose the vision, we do it so that we may attract others to join us and run with the vision.

The vision, gift or talent we have is for an appointed time; it needs time for you to expose it and let it shine. Timing is very important when it comes to serious matters like this. Pay attention to the time. No matter how long it takes, wait on the Lord because your vision will surely come to live. God does not lie; whatsoever he said in his word concerning you shall happen. God commands us to wait patiently, actively and eagerly because our dreams will surely come to live. In your time of waiting, please do not get too busy and forget to pray for your vision. Do not forget to pray because prayer makes a lot of difference.

Why should we pray for our dream, gift or vision? We need to pray because there is an enemy of progress waiting for any giving opportunity to mess things up. Do not let him win in your life. Do not let him rob you of the joy, notoriety, finance and platform that your special dream and vision can bring. If you knew what heaven knew about you and your vision, how God wants to use that to bring lasting change and bless your life, you would fast and pray for your vision every day!

There are billions of people in the world today. Have you ever wondered who else possesses all the natural endowments and privileges you have? Have you ever wondered why you have such unique gifts, such a great vision? Why you are that talented? Why it should be you and not another person? Why you are not sick, poor or broke?

If heaven prequalified you for a particular thing to do in life, that means God has found favor with you. Do not ask me why God picked you. Or if you really want to know, I must join you to ask God why he did not pick others who are better than you. After asking God this serious question, you would have given me permission to tell God to take your gift, talent or special ability from you because it is not fair. Would that be good to do? I do not think so, but I think you get the idea now. Because God chose you for such great work, please do not let heaven regret its choice by failing to perform your calling.

At the peak of Jesus' earthly ministry, on the night he was betrayed, he prayed in the garden of Gethsemane so hard when it was tough on him. It was at the time when he was about to pay the price for our sins. The moment drew closer when he would be jeered and rejected, and his body torn apart. Jesus knew what was at hand, so he went with his disciples to pray; he needed people to stand by him.

Quite interestingly, all the disciples he had taught for three years and had even sent out on internships failed him.

Instead of praying with their master, they were all sleeping, not just one time, but three times! I believe this was a disappointment for Jesus.

Jesus pleaded with the Father that if it were possible for the trial to pass over him. I know that feeling to want to escape the sacrifice and rush on stage for the glory; it happens when we have to do soul searching to see whether we are actually willing to go through the particular pain because of our vision and dream in life. Nevertheless, Jesus also prayed that it be not his will, but the will of the Father that proceeded.

Many people quit before their miracle arrives. Oh, what a disappointment to God, and our supporters! Instead of pushing hard and holding on, they throw their hands up in total defeat and walk away in shame. This is not what we should do; in our struggle to make our dreams come true, we should never give up. Rewards come only to those who refuse to quit, who continue to press on even in the midst of their deepest opposition.

When Jesus returned for the third time and saw all the disciples sleeping, he told them to watch and pray so that they would not enter into temptation. Aha, this can be a temptation to sleep at the wrong time; please do not let this happen to you because you will look stupid when you wake up later on. Sleeping at a time when people make deals and sign contracts is a very bad idea. We should never sleep in the middle of life when others are advancing and making great strides in life. We should not sleep when our pregnancy is in labor, as the pain keeps us active. Let the joy of the vision engulf our souls to bring a certain inexpressive joy.

Jesus made clear to the disciples the battle between the spirit and the flesh. The spirit is willing to yield to God and fulfill destiny; on the other hand, the body is tired and wants to quit. Please do not let your flesh override you in such critical times when we need our spirit and soul to work for our greatest good. Yield to God and fulfill your vision; let your dreams come to pass no matter what pain you must endure. Remember, quitters do not get awards; only winners do. You can be an overcomer and I can be standing there celebrating with you or getting my own award if we remain strong and pray.

This is what the Bible says about this story.

*[42]He went a little farther and fell on His face, and prayed, saying, "O My Father, if it is possible, let this up pass from Me; nevertheless, not as I will, but as You will." Then He came to the disciples and found them sleeping, and said to Peter, "What! Could you not watch with Me one hour? Watch and pray, lest you enter into temptation. The spirit indeed is willing, but the flesh is weak."* **Matthew 26:39-41 (NKJV)**

Have there been times when a lot of champions thought about quitting? Of course, yes, but they did not let it linger. They banished such thoughts from their minds and pressed hard toward their goal. Pray for your pregnancy. Pray for your dream and vision. Our world today is not fair at all. Pray for your pregnancy because not everyone who competes plays by the rules. Some people cheat, others are bullies and others bribe their way through. Pray for your vision because the devil does not want anything good to come from you and your family. Pray for your vision because the enemy would love to see your downfall and make a mockery out of you. Today I pray for you concerning your vision, dream, calling and gift in life. I pray that the Lord will fulfill his purpose in your life in the mighty name of Jesus. Amen.

## e. THE PREGNANCY IS PERSONAL

The pregnancy is personal, but the glory is general and shared. Your calling is personal. It is for you. Your vision is particular. God saw you and he saw others, yet still he picked you for that special assignment. Your vision is personal; you must treat it that way. Believe in your own vision and cherish it. The way you treat it is how others will treat it. If you are reckless about it, just forget it; others will trash it for you.

Meanwhile, be mindful because some of the people who come around may be smarter than you may be. When they see how good your vision is, yet see your recklessness towards such a valuable thing, they can come in, learn from you, take over and kick you out. This may sound odd to you, but, my friend, there are many people who have been kicked out of their own companies, churches and organizations and nobody cares about them anymore. From the day they lost their vision, their lives seem to have lost meaning. Please do not let this happen to you.

It is a terrible thing. I do not think you want to see me using your idea while you are in the unemployment line begging for rations to survive; please do not let this happen to you.

Your calling for higher heights is personal and you should treat it with care. Though Jesus prayed to the Father to take the cup of suffering, pain and agony from him, if it were possible, he recanted his statement and said to let the Father's will prevail and not his.

Until you realize that this thing has your water and blood

in it, you might not take it seriously, though it is something big. Jesus knew the glory that was at hand in spite of the reality; he said yes to the Father and endured the cross.

I must say this to you, my friend: please do not put so much faith in others who work with you such that if they do not work well or hard, things are not done. If you must work extra hours or get short-term employees or volunteers or put out more finances to cover something, just do it. This is about your vision. Make your dream come true; you have all it takes, including the endurance to take the pain of sacrifice for the sake of your vision. Just do it!

> [43]*Again, a second time, He went away and prayed, saying, "O My Father, if this cup cannot pass away from Me unless I drink it, Your will be done," And He came and found them asleep again, for their eyes were heavy.* **Matthew 26:42-43 NKJV**

## f. SACRIFICE FOR THE PREGNANCY

As you just read, Jesus had to accept paying the ultimate price for the salvation of humanity. Though in the flesh he struggled with this, his spirit and mind were ready to take on the weight. He prayed the hardest he could so that he could totally prepare himself more than ever for this great sacrifice.

> [44]*The he said to them, "My soul is exceedingly sorrowful, even to death. Stay here and watch with me."* **Matthew 26:38 NKJV**

Jesus was bold about the agony he faced. He told the disciples that his soul was exceedingly sorrowful. I want you to know that it is okay for you to express your humanity to the people you work with. It is not to show how weak you are; it is to exemplify your strength in a time of difficulty. You can acknowledge the gravity of the situation but also take courage and face the opposition. To be real is not a sign of weakness. When you state the facts but fight to overcome them, you become a champion. If you do not say how tough the situation is and you bear the pain privately, people will overlook your sacrifice, even if it is for their good.

Though Jesus told them his state of affairs, he encouraged them to stay with him to watch and pray. All of us need those special people who can stand with us in our situations; even if they cannot bear the pains with us, knowing that they are still with us will give us hope that we are actually doing something worthwhile. When things are tough, I need someone to stand with me. It makes things better.

I have gone through many things in life and at some junction I needed someone to be there with me. Though I knew that at times they did not fully understand the magnitude of the problem, their presence made a big difference. Their willingness to be with me in my lowest moments and challenging situations helped me greatly. We talked things over. We prayed together. We fasted and prayed together again and again until something good happened. These few people who stand with me in difficult times are people I can never forget. I value them so much for being there for me. I am eternally grateful to God for them.

I tell you this: when things get tough, that is when you know who loves you and who just talks about nothing. There are different types of people around us. Some people come to enjoy the fruits of our hard labor. I think one or two people just came across your mind. I call them gold diggers and honey badgers! They want the good times and nothing else. When the gold and honey run out, they get out too. Then there are others who talk good and show empathy, but that is as far as they go; they show their concern but will not do anything beyond that. They do not help. Some of the religious ones will even say, "Let's pray about it," knowing that they will not pray for you. It is the other group of people whom I love; they show concern and take the time to understand your struggle and help you. They do not run because bad times have come; they stay with you to find answers or endure pain because of the rewards ahead. I hope that you have people like that to count on when the rubber meets the road!

The Apostle Paul told the church in Philippi that we need to forget the things that are behind us and face what is ahead. We need to fix our eyes on the prize and deal with the pain of the sacrifice for the sake of our vision, dream and pregnancy. This is no time to look back, think twice forever, or wait for boardroom or hallway meetings without meaning; it is time to pull up our shirtsleeves and do something. When it is time to sacrifice for our pregnancy, we must get rid of all distractions, mount courage and cling to what is ahead. This is what the Apostle Paul taught us.

> [45]*Brethren, I do not count myself to have apprehended; but one thing I do, forgetting those things which are behind and reaching forward to those things which are ahead, I press toward the goal for the prize of the upward call of God in Christ Jesus.* **Philippians 3:13-14 NKJV**

He admits the fact that he did not figure everything out yet. Instead of fighting to bring up self-condemnation and useless worries, we need to focus on what is ahead. Nevertheless, I want to be quick to say this: this is not saying that we cannot fix some things from yesterday that we can actually fix to make the journey of life much easier.

If there were bridges we broke, we need to find a way to repair them or seek alternative routes. We need to discipline ourselves so that we do not repeat yesterday. Whatever we need to do to allow ourselves to live peaceful lives is something we need to work on diligently. If you have unsettled matters that you need to resolve, please do that right away before that little problem makes you lose good opportunities. No one knows tomorrow. Therefore, we need to settle old matters before they involve some innocent or vulnerable souls and things get out of control. There is a saying that time heals everything, but in some cases, time makes things worse. I hope you know the difference. Given time, unsettled matters make people carry resentment and grudges and sometimes plan revenge, so be careful.

Meanwhile, the Apostle Paul insisted on teaching us a valuable lesson here about being future-focused. His pitch for moving on is about being progressive and looking forward to tomorrow. For those of us who have really messed up some things yesterday, this is a good place to pay attention. It will take God himself to bail us out of yesterday's mess. When we look at the facts, the brothers and sisters we offended and how gross our offense was, even including our own family and friends, only God can save us. When we have something important to offer the world but our history is making us lose good opportunities, it is time to seek divine intervention, counseling and prayers.

Look, I know that life is not perfect, and definitely we are not perfect. Ugh, did you just say that you are not too bad compared to others? Hmm, I wonder who the others are. Oh well, I know I do it secretly in my heart sometimes to bring things closer but at the same time interpret them to my own advantage. The truth is this does not really help you or anybody else. What it does is make you put a bandage on an untreated cut; and this, my friends, is a grave danger to our health. In my other book, "Born to Take Charge", I discussed similar issue under the sections entitled "God is Not Done with Me Yet".

While that is true, I have an obligation to know myself; I need to know who I am and stop telling others what I want to be when many times it is so different from who I am right now. A humble admission about my true identity will help me begin putting together the puzzle of my life. When I am ignorant about my identity, it is so easy to claim false identities: and this is something that can be detrimental to me and to anyone who innocently comes around me.

I took it a step further and wrote at the end of the book a chapter called "Fix Me Up"; since I recognize my humanity, I need a savior to save me from all the mess. It is about being bold to God and to other wonderful people who want to help me become the best I can be.

However, if I do not know who I am or if I become arrogant about my weakness, I will not forget the past because I do not even think I have any past that needs to be left behind. If I do not know who I am, I will not do anything to improve my life; to my disgrace and loss to society, I will go around boasting about things I am not. Instead of being this ridiculous, I need to humble myself, settle the past, leave it there, enjoy every moment today and focus on tomorrow.

Yesterday is gone; we have today, and tomorrow usually brings its own affairs. Instead of beating on yourself for all your mistakes in life and become depressed, deal with the remnants of yesterday, give it to God and live your life. Pay attention to today, especially if you blundered yesterday; you need to pay double attention so that you might not repeat yesterday. We need to embrace tomorrow. The only way to do that is to lay a good foundation today so that we can have a platform upon which we can launch our dreams, visions and aspirations for life. Leave the past in the past, learn from it and move on with your life.

Forgetting the past does not mean that you fold your hands, drink beer, do illicit drugs, and run after men or women and pleasure. No, not at all. It is a time to pay attention to everything that is going on around you and to make a personal decision to make your life worthwhile.

No matter your age, size, ethnicity and financial status, you have the will to decide whether you are going to live in yesterday while today is here, robbing yourself of a tomorrow you did not properly plan. Or you can do something better by engaging yourself in something meaningful. The single most important thing to do is move on, push forward, keep doing something until your change comes. It may not be easy, but you must be strong for yourself, your family, friends and the world. No matter what pains you have to endure, do not let yesterday hold you back with its ugly paws. Fight for yourself. Fight for your dreams. Fight for your people.

Do not be one of those vulnerable people and fall prey to every little attack. Do not let the mistakes of yesterday keep you bound. Do not let yourself live in the shadow of your good life yesterday when today is in trouble. Do not let the troubles of today prevent you from focusing on tomorrow. Remember, today was yesterday's tomorrow, but now it's here. When you do not do anything good and plan for tomorrow, it too will become today's yesterday. Then, when you wake up and see all the people around you going forward in life, you will blame yourself. Get up and do something. No matter how hard life is right now, dig in there, fight hard and work towards your future. The people we call champions are people who overcame known and unknown obstacles in life. They beat the odds. You, too, can be a champion; do something.

# Part Five

## PART 5: DO THE GREATER

a. The Greater is in You
b. Recognize False Spirits and Pretenders
c. Use Discernment
d. You Can Do All Things
e. Overcome Them
f. Make the Difference Now, Not Next Time

# Do The Greater

We all are called to do something in life. Whether that something is big or small, we are required to do something meaningful with the gift of life that we have. The particular thing or things we need to do in life do not entirely rest upon us having everything before we can mount the platform of life and perform. Quite interestingly, many people, including me, are required to create our own stages and garner our audience before we can perform.

Life is very interesting. Some people get it easier in life while others suffer just to survive daily. Wherever you find yourself on the pendulum of life, whether among those who were born or grew up with silver spoons in their mouths, or those who may never see a silver spoon, you are called to articulate the call of God upon your life and do something. The thing we are called to do is nothing small, though our calling varies in size and magnitude from one person to the other; but they are all very important to make our world a better place for everyone.

God has called us to do great things; thus, we are called to *Do the Greater*. The call to *Do the Greater* is very intricate. You must handle this call with the utmost care because it is something that can make your life better, make your family better, give you money, notoriety and bless humanity at the same time! This is not a joke; it is a very serious matter. We must handle it with care because it can make us or break us. The call of God to *Do the Greater* can make others highly honor us or become very careless about us, if not disrespect us, depending on how we deal with it.

Let me be quick to kill your religious ego because the call I am talking about is not the call to ministry to serve in a church or parachurch setting alone.

No, this is a general call specific to the disciplines of life that we pursue. While the specific call to ministry is of vast importance, all the calls of God upon humanity are equally important. Actually, God intended that all of us would use our various callings to love him and serve others.

Before I became a pastor, I attended a church service where I felt insulted by the preacher when he told us that the only valuable call of God for humanity was the call to be in the gospel ministry as a pastor. It was at a time in my life when I wanted to be a medical doctor or a businessperson. This was such a blow to my life! He made me feel that other professions and disciplines we pursue in life are not so important or necessary.

How can being a businessman, employing people, including church members who will later care for their families, send their kids to school, go to church, pay tithes and offerings, not be important to God? Most of the people in the church, even in that service, were selling petite market to survive. How can being a medical doctor catering to the community and making people healthy not be important to God? I began to wonder whether that pastor knew that there are people, medical doctors, doctors who are ministers, who travel the world with their staff doing medical missions, saving lives and souls for the Lord Jesus Christ. I had such a great problem with his premise. There was such discontentment in my soul and spirit as soon as he said that. My spirit testified to the Spirit of God that this pastor had a very naïve and limited vision of the call of God. As he talked, the Lord opened my spirit and began to pour into me things about his call that were already at work in me, including that the pastor was not talking about it in a fair manner. Let me be quick to say that I did not disagree with him that the call of God to the gospel ministry is not important; no, but to say that it is the single most important call of all calls – that was my problem.

As he continued to preach, God told me that he has given a diversity of calls to humankind and every call is of great importance. There is always a problem, a lack, a situation in our world when someone does not fulfill his or her calling in life. It leaves a vacuum that God has to use others to fill – no wonder others have multiple calls! God told me that it was his call that made someone build the house the pastor lived in, paved the road he walked on to go to church, fabricated and sewed the clothes he wore and even printed the Bible from which he preached. The electricity we used was his call and the clean, filtered pump water we drank were other calls. If he called some into the gospel ministry with different calls to be apostles, prophets, pastors, teachers, healers, workers of miracles and so forth, how much more is his call to the whole wide world? It must be as big as the world!

As God has called some to be prophets, apostles, pastors, workers of miracles and so forth, he has also called others to be scientists, medical doctors, engineers, pilots, computer geeks, politicians, authors, sportsmen, entertainers, mothers and the list goes on. The call of God upon our lives is about fulfilling a particular thing that heaven knows the world needs to make things better. Before electricity was discovered, people used fire and other things for light and heat.

Today, we cannot imagine a world without electricity because almost everything we do is powered by it. Only a few things are manual and solar. Somebody gave us cars, some brothers gave us airplanes, somebody gave us computers, the internet, telephones, streetlights, mailboxes, etc. I think you get the idea. People are using their gifts, talents and abilities, their callings, to give something good for everyone to use. What about you and me?

Bill Gates gave us computers and Microsoft, Steve Jobs gave us Apple computers and the iPhone, Mark Zuckerberg gave us Facebook; what about you? If the others can use their natural talents, gifts and abilities to *Do the Greater*, how much more are those who possess spiritual gifts supposed to do to improve our world?

Or are those with spiritual gifts turning this thing inward and focusing on personal aggrandizement and not concerned about people and the future? Are they taking the gift of God as a personal thing for fame and riches when the world around them is begging, crying and dying because of lack? Whether you possess a natural gift or a spiritual gift, all of us are called to *Do the Greater* and make the most of every opportunity to build, improve and conserve.

*Do the Greater* will give you an in-depth understanding of how saying yes to the call of God upon your life can make you somebody; not just to be the best you can be, but to do something that will help others and make our world a better place for us and our children. Let me ask you, what do you have to give to the world?

## a. THE GREATER IS INSIDE YOU

All of us have the God-factor in us to create. According to the Bible in the Book of Beginnings, Genesis, God commanded everything that exists today in motion. God commanded light to be and there was light. God instructed the light to divide into day and night forever, and it did. God commanded a divide between land and skies, and it happened. He commanded the world to give water; the sky and the land both gave water. Then God commanded the water to redistribute itself into oceans, seas, rivers, creeks, lakes and ravines, and it happened. He made the water of the ocean and seas salt water, but the water of the rivers, creeks, ravines and most lakes fresh water – what a God we serve!

I am not here to bore you with the biblical account of the creation story, but I am driving somewhere. After God made all things that make life possible, he commanded plants and animals in their varieties and pairs to be, and yes they were. Yet, after all the activity, God said it was now time to make man in his image and likeness – thus, he made mankind! When God made man, he made him in his image and likeness. That means because God is a creator, we have components to create; it is in our DNA. We bear the characteristics of God. We have free will – the ability to choose between right and wrong, the ability that makes love possible. We are not some robots controlled by mechanics; we are human – a powerful entity. We have the ability to love and judge; love becomes the highest human value. When we love, we show care, support, improvement, companionship and so forth. Love, in its purest sense, is not possible in the absence of free will because we would not be able to choose whom and what we love. We would all be controlled by mechanics.

Now, if it is true that we are made in the image and likeness of God and that we possess free will and the ability to participate in love, God expects us to manifest that. Besides, the Bible teaches us that God blessed us and gave us charge over our world to control things in the three known spheres – land, water and air. God has given us the full duty charge to be blessed, bear fruit, multiply, fill the earth, subdue it and exert dominion. As I think about how unique we are to God and this world, I need to fully understand the magnitude of our existence. Definitely, we are not just here to eat, sleep, reproduce and die someday; we are called to cater to the world, tame it and govern it accordingly.

*Do the Greater* is a stern reminder of what is already on the inside of us that needs to come out and shine. It is a command to fulfill our calling and use our gifts, talents and abilities with the utmost respect and care. We are not losers or victims of circumstances. We are not mere people with inabilities; no, we are great people made and given charge to take our full leadership position and take charge of the world. The way God has set up things indicates that if we do not do something, something might happen that could affect us and make our world an unfriendly place to live. I think when you look around, you can see what our silence, fear and reluctance brought upon us today; and that is not good at all.

I am glad to tell you that you and I have on the inside of us the God-factor, that special thing that sets the human species apart from the rest of creation. We have the character of God and the possibility of knowing the will of God for our lives and this world. Do not be the person who sits down and does nothing when there is a lot to do. Do not be the one who complains all day long when you are supposed to be the head and leader somewhere; do something.

Every time you see a need in society, remember that this thing is the unfulfilled calling of some lazy or rebellious person. This is the work of a very selfish person, a person who wants to make the graveyard more talented than our community. Such people are full of unused potential. We all need to do something to make our world a better place. I suggest that if anyone, I mean anyone, does not work to fulfill his or her portion in life, that person does not deserve to enjoy the hard labor of others; such people deserve to be punished.

When you do not fulfill your calling in life, you are a thief! How so? I will tell you. Your refusal to use your gifts, talents and abilities will rob you of the leadership role that was meant for you. It will make you lose your place in society as somebody who contributed to our world to make it a better place. When this happens, you cheat yourself out of money you could be making, rob yourself of the rights and privileges such a position brings; ultimately, you rob God of the joy in seeing you being obedient and prosperous in life! Now, this is what makes you a thief, a cheater, a rogue, and a dangerous consumer without productivity! Such people need to be dragged to court and punished publicly.

Let us dig in a little more; here is a reference in the Bible of what the Apostle John said.

*[46]You, dear children, are from God and have overcome them, because the one who is in you is greater than the one who is in the world.* **I John 4:4 NIV**

As the children of God, we have overcome the adversary; because those who are from God are greater than those who are just of this world by far. One of the greatest failures of humanity is to not subdue the enemy and exercise our dominion properly. If what God said in the beginning is true, that he blessed us and gave us the power to be fruitful, multiply, fill the earth, subdue it and have dominion, then you and I must do something to exert proper power and authority over our territory.

Our territory is land, water, air and everything within it, so anything or anyone here is under our rule. If things and people threaten our peaceful rule and we do not send them a stern message that trespassers will be prosecuted to the fullest extent of the law, they can walk all over us because there are no consequences. There are some people and things that are frisky and want to test our resolve.

They want to see whether we have the discipline to protect our domain. They want to test our rules and push boundaries. We need to send them warnings, if not preemptive strikes, to tell them that we are in charge.

To be frank, knowing what happened to mankind in the beginning, I believe that God is disappointed in us every time we let people and things infringe upon our rights. The truth is, God did not let us get away with our disobedience and challenge to his authority; he disciplined us accordingly. So now why will we, who should have learned from the Father, loosely rule and let infiltrators occupy our domain? This is what I think is one of our biggest failures before God.

You are from God and I am from God. We have in us what it takes to overcome the enemy that wants to delay our progress, destroy us and kill us. We can win this battle. In the gospel of John, the Bible states that:

> [47]*The thief does not come except to steal, and to kill, and to destroy. I have come that they may have life, and that they may have it more abundantly.* **John 10:10 NKJV**

We have to understand that there is an enemy who does not relent; this enemy is bent on destruction either by false friendship, manipulation, direct attacks or some other sneaky way. The enemy is not your friend.

He comes only to steal, kill and destroy. We have to ask ourselves, what is it that the adversary wants from us? Is it our money, health, vehicles, clothes, spouses or kids? No, none of those! Then why is the enemy pursuing us to steal from us, kill and destroy us? What does he really want? I will tell you, and I think you will be surprised.

The enemy does not care about your people and properties; no, not that at all! What the enemy cares about, the reason he is behind you day and night, is the Word of God in your life. It is about the dream, the vision and purpose God has given you.

The Word of God in you will cause you to fulfill your mission in life, and when you fulfill your purpose for living, the world will be a better place. That thing God has created you for will build something new or improve on something to help humanity and bring glory to the name of God.

When you and I understand our vision and purpose and fulfill them, there will not be famine, because we will provide food for the hungry.

When we fulfill our mission in life, we will end poverty because we will establish self-help initiatives and other programs to empower people and make them financially stable. When we fulfill our calling in life, there will not be terrible diseases, especially curable diseases that kill masses of poor people. There will not be other terrible sicknesses that kill anyone, especially sicknesses that are engineered in laboratories by pharmaceutical companies to make millions by gambling with the lives of innocent people around the world.

When we fulfill our purpose in life, we will end corruption because there will be God-fearing leaders who will take leadership and serve their constituents with love and care, always seeking the interests of their people. When we fulfill our portion in life, banks and other financial institutions will not hike prices and cause a recession to make more money illegally as masses of people lose their homes, vehicles, businesses and livelihoods.

This, is the reason the devil, our chief adversary, plots against your life – so you can be irrelevant to God because you lost your purpose. When you lose your purpose in life, you become a vagabond, a useless person. The devil is not afraid of churches. He has corrupted many pastors, bishops, apostles, prophets and prayer people by making them add juju, voodoo and witchcraft to their ministries so that they can have power, people and money and work miracles.

Do not let miracles carry you away; some of them have a price behind them that you have to pay later. These corrupt ministers will go to the extent of making sacrifices of animals and people to become strong. They are so caught up in their ways and they protect their eating grounds. Now, let me ask you this: if even the church can be corrupt like this, what can they say to corrupt politicians and other leaders? The answer is simple – nothing, because all of them are doing the same thing. Beware!

## b. RECOGNIZE FALSE SPIRITS AND PRETENDERS

As we embark on the journey to *Do the Greater*, we need to understand that there are people out there who do not play by the rules. They are not fair. They lie, cheat, scandalize, kill or do whatsoever they can do to rob us of our place in the lineup of things. We need to tell those imposters and wicked people that we are not easy prey; we are not soft targets. It is because of such people that the Bible stated in Genesis that we must subdue them if we want to be in that special leadership role for which God has called us.

*[48]Then God blessed them, and God said to them, "Be fruitful and multiply; fill the earth and subdue it; have dominion over the fish of the sea, over the birds of the air, and over every living thing that moves on the earth."* **Genesis 1: 28 NKJV**

God has commanded us to subdue everything that wants to get out of bounce. We are stewards and we need to handle God's creation and his affairs with diligence and care. We have the power and authority to subdue every person, thing, living or nonliving, place and spirit to submit to our will. We need to use our power in the Lord to find, arrest, prosecute and condemn every force that threatens our peaceful rule. Whether they come as pretenders or bold attackers, we need to put them in the place they belong – under our feet. We need to test every spirit, every prophecy against the Word of God.

For those of you running after prophets and prayer people here and there, please make sure you know that they are of God. Our world today is getting so unsafe and so wicked that even pastors, prophets and prayer people are adding other things to their ministries to have the power to perform miracles. Please be careful to whom you offer your head to lay hands on or anoint you; make sure they are a Bible-believing man or woman of God and not some joker pretending to be real. In the past, a lot of these people were easily recognizable by their red or white garments, but these days, they are wearing expensive suits and nice dresses. Do not let the beauty of their church buildings, their number of attendees, or their flamboyance fool you. People are desperate these days to make a name for themselves and make a few bucks too. Test the spirit before you become a victim.

*[49]Beloved, do not believe every spirit, but test the spirits to see whether they are from God, for many false prophets have gone out into the world.* **I John 4: 1 ESV**

There are pretenders and imposters everywhere in our world today. They are in the church, in politics, schools, business, science, social things and everywhere. These imposters lie, corrupt people and lead masses into destruction. God warned us to be very careful about them. As you are busy living your life and fulfilling your call, you must properly secure all your valuables before you become a victim.

Do not let the enemy destroy all of your hard work to build your life, family, education, business, church or whatever you do. Beware of false spirits, pretenders and imposters who come as angels but are actually savage demons. Do not let their appearance, smooth talk and show carry you into destruction. They are not your friend, family or partner; they come only to steal, kill and destroy.

It is because of this that the Apostle John said we should test every spirit to see whether it comes from God. Some spirits, people or things do not come from God, even though they may disguise themselves to look that way; but they are not of God. They are of the devil and on a mission to destroy you.

Please do not help them succeed in destroying your good life; you are valuable to God, to your family, friends and the world. That is why we need to test every spirit to see if it lines up with the Word of God. You must know how to recognize these pundits before they lead you astray or destroy your life. There is a way to determine if a spirit or prophecy, pastor or prayer person is from God. This is what the Bible says:

*50By this you know the Spirit of God: every spirit that confesses that Jesus Christ has come in the flesh is from God, and every spirit that does not confess that Jesus is not from God. This is the spirit of the antichrist, which you heard was coming and now is in the world already.* **I John 4:2-3 ESV**

I know many people usually ask how we are supposed to know who is real or fake; well, there it is. Thank you for asking. By their confession of the Lord Jesus Christ, you can tell whether they are of God or not. For the most part, you do not even have to be strong in the things of God to notice that something is wrong when you are around such people. They seem to talk more about themselves and praise themselves than they talk about the Lord Jesus Christ. They talk as if they themselves have the power to work miracles. They are quick to threaten people because they use fear to control people and rob them or have their way with them sexually.

I heard the story of a so-called prophet who has a pool in his yard and tells all the women looking for deliverance or husbands to bathe naked in his pool with him, one by one. He tells them that they must hug him so he can pray for the spirit to get inside of them. When the naked women hug him, he will then begin to rub their body, caress them and soon after start kissing them and have sex with them as a way for the power of God to come into them. And, by the way, each of these women has to pay a stiff offering of $50 USD before the pool prayer session. Imagine that! He collects $50 USD, lies to them about miracles and then has sex with them in the pool in his yard. Sadly, the place can be so packed with women who are desperate for men and miracles.

Another pastor, who does not even have an office at his church, will tell all the women seeking children or husbands and other miracles to come for special prayers on the altar behind a curtain. I guess he was instituting the *"Holy of Holies"* in his own right. Behind that curtain in the church, he tells the women to strip naked so that he, the "holy spirit", can put the babies in them, or so that he can prepare them for their soon-to-be husbands. This so-called pastor have sex with the women in the church, on the altar, until one day he messed with the wrong man's wife. This man was a soldier.

As the story goes, they suffered from infertility and were seeking medical help for a solution as well as seeking the face of God. The couple went to a Bible-believing church, but it was desperation that took his wife to this *"Mr. Solution*

*Master"*, as I will call him. This so-called pastor was in the habit sleeping with the women who wanted children and husbands in the name of God. Somehow, some of the women said they got their miracles. It was because of such false testimonies that this woman went there to seek the face of God, too.

As usual, after consultation, she paid a fee and proceeded to see the man of God already waiting on the altar for prayer and sex. As the so-called pastor began to pray for her, he began to touch her in all the wrong places in the name of the Spirit being at work. However, the woman was not one of his regular victims; she began to resist his kisses and rubbing. She screamed, saying that she did not want that, she wanted only prayers. He insisted that the woman had to be respectful and sensitive to the leading of the spirit.

He talked her down until she agreed to have sex with him. In the meantime, her husband came home early from work and began looking for her. Somebody in their yard told him that she had gone for prayers at that church. Having heard funny stories about this pastor and his church, the husband ran to the place to get his wife out of there before something happened. He was five minutes late; this fake pastor was already enjoying his wife. When the man got to the church, he asked to see the pastor because his wife had come for prayers, but the assistants told him to wait, as the pastor was in serious prayer for somebody.

As soon as he heard this, he pushed his way through the doors and entered the church; to his surprise the church was empty. As he was about to turn around and leave, he heard funny noises from behind the curtain on the altar. He quickly ran there to see what was happening, and to his utmost surprise, this pastor was having sex with his wife. The man slapped the pastor so hard that he immediately fell off his wife; the man covered his wife and beat the devil out of the pastor.

The pastor's assistants came to his aid, but the soldier was too much for all of them. He beat the pastor so hard that he broke his nose and give him a black eye before the neighbors came and pulled them apart. The news spread that night about the pastor and the church; by the next morning, the pastor had run away and the church was closed. Bravo, good soldier!

There is a myriad of stories I can tell you about fake, corrupt and dangerous pastors. They are involved in lies, scandal, fraud, constant adulteries, voodoo and witchcraft; some of them go to the extent of doing both animal and human sacrifices just to be strong, do miracles and get money.

One other fake prophetess who tries to force herself in the ministry uses her witchcraft mother to see visions and make miracles for people. When an unsuspecting person comes in for prayers and explains their story, she will tell them to come back the next day because she wants to pray for them. As the person leaves, she will call her mother in Africa and explain their story; the mother will then invoke their spirit in Africa to see them and tell her exactly what to do.

When the person returns, she tells them whatever the mother told her; after collecting money, the mother will control the results from Africa, producing fake miracles. Open your eyes!

When God made us he put a personal security check within us that tells us when something is not right; it is the spirit of discernment. Each one of us needs to learn how to use it to protect ourselves and our families.

It is not that all the men and women of God are fake and dangerous, no; there are great ministers of the gospel out there. I tell you this so that you will know how to take good care of yourself. God has called you to become somebody great; I do not want you to fall prey to anybody's scheme.

## c.  USE DISCERNMENT

So, how will we differentiate false spirits and pastors from true ones?  Let us review our answers so far.  This is what the Apostle John said about these spirits and people who pretend to come from God but are not really of God.

*[51]Beloved, do not believe every spirit, but test the spirits to see whether they are from God, for many false prophets have gone out into the world.  By this you know the Spirit of God: every spirit that confesses that Jesus Christ has come in the flesh is from God, and every spirit that does not confess that Jesus is not from God.  This is the spirit of the antichrist, which you heard was coming and now is in the world already.* **1 John 4: 1-3 ESV**

The Apostle John tells us to watch the place of the Lord Jesus Christ in their lives and ministries.  Is it all about them or about God and the saving grace of Christ Jesus?  If they are of God, Jesus Christ will be the center of everything they say and do; if it is not so, that is a red flag.  Beware.  While this is true, it is just the first part.  Some of these fake pastors, prophets and prayer people are subtle; they know how to hide their clandestine moves and appear to be good.  Thank God there is another way to detect the group that will pass under the radar; we can still catch them.

The Apostle Paul knew firsthand what false spirits and false prophets and pastors were because they were around in his day.  Some of them even tried to lead his congregations astray.  That is why each of us needs to pay keen attention and take appropriate action.  Even Jesus himself warned us about these sorts of spirits and people. We need to be careful with them. Let us pay attention and behave well.

*⁵²For as many as are led by the Spirit of God, these are sons of God. The Spirit Himself bears witness with our spirit that we are children of God, and if children, then heirs – heirs of God and joint heirs with Christ, if indeed we suffer with Him, that we may also be glorified together.* **Romans 8:14,16 &17 NKJV**

The Apostle Paul tells us here that to become children of God, we must be led by the Spirit of God; not just any other spirit – not our spirit, nor any strange spirit of man-made gods or devils. This is so important to help us understand any person or thing we deal with. We need to know and understand what drives them and empowers them. If you are a true child of God, the Spirit of God is within you and will direct your path. If you want to know how this works, just check the things you do and say and the places you go; you will be your own judge.

Let us do a little exercise. I want you to think about the things you said over the last few days, the things you did and the places you went. Do you think Jesus Christ would be pleased with them? By giving an honest answer to this question, you are examining yourself to see if your life right now makes you a good child of God. The same can be applied to pastors, prophets and prayer people. We can see by their livelihoods in the community whether they are of God or not.

The second part of this is very important. The Spirit of God testifies or bears witness to our spirit that we are of God. How can anyone determine whether a pastor, prophet, bishop or prayer person is real? Well, when your spirit is right with God, or many times for your own protection, God uses our natural instincts, known as our gut feelings, to help us see the truth. Meanwhile, for all those who are filled with the Spirit of God, a certain uneasiness will come upon you. Sometimes you will hear the audible voice of God speaking to you and you will know that something about that atmosphere is not right.

The Apostle Paul says that we are joint heirs with the Lord Jesus Christ. So if you see a preacher or prayer person leaving their partner Jesus behind and operating as if they are on their own, take caution. Jesus is the center of the church, the chief cornerstone, so leaving him behind to operate solo means that something is not right at all.

The next part of the verse said that we will suffer with Christ. Ah, this is very important. Fake pastors, prophets and prayer people do not ever want to suffer for the sake of Jesus Christ; they just want to enjoy and enjoy and enjoy, even things and people that do not belong to them. Pastors and prayer people like this want money before people can talk to people. They want a guaranteed amount of money or things before and after they pray. Sometimes they will have sex with those who come for prayers. Shame on them!

We, as the people of God, suffer many times at the hands of our unsaved friends and family because of Jesus Christ; how much more are pastors supposed to bear the scars of the ministry? Jesus Christ went here and there preaching and teaching and suffered a violent death in our place.

However, he said that in taking up our cross, there would be tough times we would have to endure and overcome. So, if a so-called pastor, prophet or prayer person is in it only for the honey, you should check them out. The Apostle Paul boasted about his beatings, prison time and chains because of Christ, yet some of these so-called men and women of God want only the enjoyment. They make people fast and pray for their problems while they go home and eat well before coming back to the church to pray. Some of them will even flip a little bottle before coming in to pray; no wonder they have so much energy to scream and bounce here and there, sweating.

In this section, I talked a lot about phony pastors, prophets and prayer people, but not all these fake people are church people. Some of them are in the marketplace; from politicians to community leaders to bankers, they are everywhere. They are teachers, co-workers, family members and close friends. I would now love to address the issue of fake people, pretenders and imposters. Due to their multiplicity in different areas of life, we need to be very careful. When we wake up in the morning, we need to be like Jesus Christ himself and commit our day to the hands of God before we go out. The Bible teaches us that,

*[53]Very early in the morning, while it was still dark, Jesus got up, left the house and went off to a solitary place, where he prayed.* **Mark 1:35 NIV**

Commit your day into the hands of the Lord and He will guide your heart. The Lord will keep you away from imposters or help you overcome their tricks. If Jesus woke up in the morning to pray before beginning his day, you and I need to pray as well. I really think you and I need to pray more for the power of God to come alive in us wherever we go.

We need to pray before we go to bed because people do evil under the cover of darkness. Some of them spend their time discussing you and me and plot against us. We have to pray and commit our families and our properties to the hands of the Lord and declare that no weapon formed against us shall prosper. You have to declare it upon your life, upon your man or woman and upon your children, business, church and activities. The devil is busy prowling around, looking for whom to devour; do not let it be you.

*[54]One of those days Jesus went out to a mountainside to pray, and spent the night praying to God.* **Luke 6:12 NIV**

The Bible teaches us that Jesus went somewhere to pray alone all night. He prayed in the night. The night can be heavy, full of a lot of things, so we need to pray. The Bible says about evil people that,

*55They lie awake at night, hatching sinful plots. Their actions are never good. The make no attempt to turn from evil.* **Psalm 36:4 NLT**

Evil people are busy at night; they plot evil under the cover of darkness to harm you and me. We do not have to fall victim to their scheme; like Jesus Christ, let us pray at night and commit our families to the Lord in prayer. Pray for your man or women; pray for your children and friends. Pray for your colleagues and pray for your community and the nations. Your prayer has so much power to divert evil. By the way, you are not the only one praying. As you pray, the Lord raises others to pray in similar directions. Therefore, you can pray with confidence knowing that the Lord has an army of people defending his cause in your community and in your nation. All you and I have to do is our part.

Again, let me say this: there are evil people out there, some of whom pretend to be what they are not. There are people out there who are against your life and would do anything to destroy you, steal from you or kill you. I am not ready to die yet, especially not at the hands of some scumbag, no way! I do not think you should die before your time, either. We need to continue to live our lives and even someday work together on projects that will make us money and help others. I am so into you to the extent that I pray for you, that the Lord will guide you and protect you against all invaders, imposters and direct attackers.

You were born to subdue. All power and authority to protect your domain lie in your hands and in your mouth.

Use the Word of God properly to protect your life and your stuff. Join me and let us work together and help others rise up to be the men and women of honor they need to be to lift people to the next level and protect what is dear to them. This, I tell you, my friend, is a great undertaking. There are many people today who are victims of fake pastors, prophets and prayer people.

They have lost their money and integrity to the craftiness and wickedness of their so-called men and women of God. Let us stand up against the other fake people, imposters, pretenders and wicked people who are hurting people in our communities. You can teach somebody today so that they will not lose their identity to thieves and scavengers. God bless you. Let us help one another as much as we can. There are some people who cannot help themselves; it will take you and me to stand up for them. I trust you will do so because humanity demands it.

### d. DO ALL THINGS

If what the Bible says about God is true, that all things are possible with God, and if it is also true that to them that believe all things are possible, that means you and I can exceedingly *Do the Greater* and fulfill our purpose in life. We can *Do The Greater* beyond our wildest imaginations! Let me remind you of what God said to us in the beginning of time. This is what we have and what we are capable of:

*56Then God blessed them, and God said to them, "Be fruitful and multiply; fill the earth and subdue it; have dominion over the fish of the sea, over the birds of the air, and over every living thing that moves on the earth."*
**Genesis 1: 28 NKJV**

When you wake up every morning, tell yourself that you are blessed, your husband or wife is blessed, your children are blessed, your friends are blessed, your business, work or ministry is covered with blessings because God said that we are blessed. God has given us blessings in every area of our lives, but we must declare those blessings and work towards them so that they can happen to us. I want my bank account to be blessed. You and I must remind ourselves and declare to the devil that we are the blessed children of God, and that anything else to make us less than we are will not be tolerated.

God did not just bless us without giving us specifics about the blessings he conferred upon us. He pronounced blessings on our heads to bear fruit, to multiply, to fill the earth, to subdue it and have dominion over everything on the land, in the water and in the air. Oh wow, I can see the blessings of God all around me in this place. Sometimes conditions make us not see and appreciate the bountiful blessings of God, but I challenge you to truly put your trust in God and you will see that what now confronts you as a problem is only a stepping stone to your miracle. It is a platform of performance you just need to fix; definitely, it is a ladder to your divine lifting. All you need to do is ask God in faith to make it stand properly.

We can do all things in Christ Jesus! It makes me wonder whether many Christians know their God at times when they question and criticize another Christian who is taking a bold step to do something bigger than what they did before. If the Bible says we can dream big, have faith and apply work, and the God of miracles will give us the desires of our hearts, why are believers jeering fellow believers who take God at his word?

I want to talk to all the dreamers out there. Whether this is your first notable project or you are going from one to the other, do not listen to the naysayers; all they do is talk and talk and talk. Some of them are just jealous of you because they condemn themselves and do not believe that God can use them mightily as he is about to do with you.

When the people who should pray for you and support you financially and morally become your first critics, I want you to know that God is up to something big in your life. It is the devil who employs them to attack you with bad words and sometimes scandal.

I must say this to you: you are a big girl or boy, so do not let the useless talk of those with no direction for their own lives stop what God is about to do in your life.

Do not listen to them. Do not fight them; just become true to yourselves and focus on what the Lord has called you to do. There may be times you need to be affirmative and settle scores with one or two instigators.

When you are doing this, gather all the facts, pray about it and do it big without relenting. That will send a good message to anyone who dares open his or her mouth to talk crap; you will truly silence them.

Let us continue. After the flood, God reminded man about his commitment to putting man in charge of the world. This is what God said with a twist.

*57 The fear and dread of you will fall on all the beasts of the earth, and on all the birds in the sky, on every creature that moves along the ground, and on all the fish in the sea; they are given into your hands.* **Genesis 9:2 NIV**

In Genesis 1:28, the Bible said that we should subdue everything and exercise our dominion. Quite interesting, according to what we just read above, God made it easier for us by putting the fear and dread of us upon all the animals, fish and birds in their classes. Animals on land, fish in the water and birds in the sky in their variations must submit to our rule. What an awesome God we serve! No wonder today man is able to tame the wild animals and make them pets for our comfort and entertainment.

I want you to think about the significance of Genesis 1:28 and Genesis 9:2. In here we learned that God gave us power and authority over everything, including all living and nonliving things, plants and animals and anything in between. From the things that are on land, to those in the water and on to the things in the air, they are all given to us to govern.

If we control land, water and air, we have full control and authority over our territory because we control all three spheres of existence. This means that we control things in all states: air, liquid and gas. We control all things. We can speak to any living creature and it will understand our language. I love this!

Therefore, the next time who see your mom, aunt, uncle, girlfriend, boyfriend or anybody else for that matter hurling insults at you and telling you that you are nothing, tell them that you are not just something, you are everything! You are everything because God has given you power and authority over land, water and air and everything in it; if that person does not see your importance, it is to your gain and their ultimate loss.

You do not have to fight. Just make this bold statement and walk away; if this is the last thing they ever hear from you, make sure they hear it well so that they can regret and cry later when they see God bringing out your true value and blessing your life.

Many times it is self-condemnation, not just curses from others or the devil, that keeps us down. You have to love yourself. I love myself. I love myself very much. It is by my love for self that I measure the love I have for others. Oh no, do not get me wrong; I am not selfish. It is a biblical principle, and this comes from Jesus Christ.

*⁵⁸"Teacher, which is the greatest commandment in the Law?" Jesus replied: "Love the Lord your God with all your heart and with all your soul and with all your mind. This is the first and greatest commandment. And the second is like it, 'Love your neighbor as yourself.' All the Law and the Prophets hand on these two commandments."* **Matthew 22:36-40 NIV**

Jesus was asked about the greatest commandment over all the over commandments, and he said, in short, love God and love people like you love yourself. We must first love God with everything in us; and if we do that, it will make us love others. But how are we to love others and by what do we measure this love for others? If it is true that we really love God, his love will make us love other people. I want to be frank and tell you this: if you do not love yourself, you cannot love anyone else. You will just be using people and hurting them.

Learn to love yourself because it is from your self-love that you will love others. Do not allow anybody to look down upon you and let it stick on you; send it back to the sender and walk away. You are that good and wonderful to God, but you must learn to exercise your power and authority properly: love God, love yourself and love others.

I know there are others who say that this is too much. Oh no, just listen to what the Apostle Paul has to say.

*⁵⁹ I can do all things through Christ who strengthens me.* **Philippians 4:13 NKJV**

The Apostle Paul said that he could do all things, not because of his physical strength, mental capacity, ability, education, money, family or connections. No, rather, he said he could do all things through the Lord Jesus Christ who gave him strength. I too can say, I can do all things through Christ who gives me strength. It is not on my own, but my strength, success, growth and uplifting come from the Lord. This is the sort of thinking we should all have.

You are who you are today because the Lord kept you. It is not because of your smartness or a man or woman who helped you. It is because the Lord is with you, even in times when you do not see him at work. There is an unseen hand that is making things happen in your life; that hand is pushing you forward and passing you through difficult situations. You are not on your own. Jesus Christ is with you.

Because of the purpose of God in your life, you will make it in life. Our brother Job said that,

> [60] *"I know that you can do all things; no purpose of yours can be thwarted.* **Job 42:2 NIV**

Let me be quick to say this: while I may not know how the Lord will bless my life and bless your life, we can rest assured that the purpose of the Lord in our lives will come to pass. The God of wonders will move things in my direction and in your direction to bring about our miracles. I have the grace to understand that I do not have to know how God works every detail of my blessings before I can receive them. No, all I have to do is trust God and obey him and we will work together to give me the future he promised. I want you to also work diligently with God, trust him and work with him to create a blessing beyond your own expectations.

> [61] *As you do not know the path of the wind, or how the body is formed in a mother's womb, so you cannot understand the work of God, the Maker of all things.* **Ecclesiastes 11:5 NIV**

I do not understand everything in our natural world. How can ask I God to figure out everything concerning my life before I receive my blessings? No, I am not going to do that. I will let God be God while I remain me.

While we can seek knowledge and acquire great things, I cannot claim to understand the intricacies of life and of this world because I do not understand everything. What I should pursue in life is understanding the will of God for my life and working with him to give me my portion in life and to help me fulfill my purpose.

When you and I began to work with God, we will not bother about who and what God uses to bring our miracles; our concerns will rather be walking in the ways of God to experience our miracles. God is the maker of all things and knows how to make things work in our favor.

We can do all things through Christ Jesus who gives us strength. Do not live to the expectations of the wicked people and naysayers who want to see you sick, poor or in trouble. Work with God to help you become what you are called to become in life. You can do all things and I can do all things because it is not by my power or might, but rather it is by the Spirit of the living God.

I pray that God will wake you up from any sleep you are in and set you on your way to becoming somebody great. You can make it. I can make it. You will make it. I will make it. We are going to make it not because of who we are or who we know, but rather, because God gives us strength so that we can *Do the Greater* and accomplish great things in life.

You have it in you to become a leader, a champion and a world changer. Do not let any plebian intimidate you; they need to submit to you or get special treatment for rude people. May the Lord give you strength to overcome your weakness. May God bless the sweat from your brow. May God bless the work of your hands. May your ideas blossom. I would love to see the glory of the Lord upon your life, so keep me in the loop.

### e. OVERCOME THEM

Because of the great God inside, no demon, no witch, no devil, no evil spirit, no evil person, place or thing can destroy the purpose of God in your life. You will overcome them one by one, group by group because the hand of the Lord is upon you. Some of the battles you do not even need to fight; the Lord will fight for you. Whatever thing, person or place stands against your life and wants to steal from you, destroy you or kill you shall not prevail in the name of Jesus Christ. I stand in the power and authority of God and command them to be destroyed by the power of the Holy Spirit in Jesus' name. Wherever they gather against you, they shall fall; they shall never prevail against you. You will overcome them one by one, group by group because the hand of the Lord is upon you.

The Apostle John said this about you,

*[62]You, dear children, are from God and have overcome them, because the one who is in you is greater than the one who is in the world.* **I John 4:4 NIV**

As the children of God, we have special security. Our security is not there just to protect us, but is there to overcome every adversity. The Bible declares that,

*[63]No weapon formed against you shall prosper, and every tongue which rises against you in judgment you shall condemn. This is the heritage of the servants of the Lord, and their righteousness is from me," says the Lord.* **Isaiah 54:17 NKJV**

I love this so much. I do not have to live under fear in the night because of evil people. I do not have to worry whether I will make it through the day and come home safely to my family because the Lord is with me. I can rest assured that no weapon of malicious talk, conniving, evil plots and witchcraft against my life, family, business, church and things shall prosper in the name of Jesus. No matter how hard they try to take me down, I will still remain standing because God is on my side. I love the second part of this verse. It says that every tongue that dares open its mouth to talk evil about me, spoil my name, tarnish my good reputation, hurl curses upon my life, I – not the Lord – shall condemn.

God says he will stop the heavy weapons against your life and against my life, but the liars, those gossipers, those busybodies, aha, we can handle them. We need to stand on the word of God and pack them where they belong – under our feet. Do not just sit back and let any loser say negative things to you for them to stick; send them right back to the sender with a bonus.

If somebody tells you that you will suffer in life or you will not make it, tell them, oh no, this is the wrong address. I will make it in life. I will prosper; not just me, but all my children and me. By the way, when I start my new business, you will be my employee, and if you continue to piss me off, I will fire you without pay. Tell them, "Your curse or witch cannot touch me; now I reverse it and repackage it and send it right back to you double. Whatsoever wicked thing you plan for my life, let it happen to you even more so severely in the name of Jesus Christ." Then when you are finished, say Amen! And it shall be accomplished.

The last part of this verse says that this is the heritage of the Lord. What does this mean? Total security is our heritage in the Lord. Peace, joy and stability are our portion in the Lord. Do not ever sit back and let some evil people say bad things about you and your family. Send it right back to them. Send it right to them, my friend. Do not let it stay with you; just send it back to the sender.

Many times we become too nice to evil people who want to steal from us, destroy our lives and kill us. That is not good at all. I think God must be disappointed in us when we sit back and let evil people walk all over us. No, we should do our best and stand on the word of God and take charge of our lives and defend our family and properties. We need to go ahead and defend those who have nobody. Do not ever let the devil mess with your family and friends when you have the power of God alive and well in your life.     Look, God is waiting for you to make a move. Heaven is watching whether you will make yourself a victim or let God be glorified in the situation by standing up and declaring the word of God to every evil thing that threatens your peace. The warring angels are on guard, ready for the attack; they are just waiting for you to put them into action. Jesus Christ and God the Father are watching to see if you and I will wake up from our sleep, mount the stage, subdue the enemy and exercise authority over our domain. Do something today to make God proud by becoming the man or woman of substance you are. Stand up for what is right and do not let the devil and some losers mess with you.

The Bible teaches us that we have powerful weapons of war that we can deploy at will. I am using my own. Please find yours and use it properly. Hear what the Apostle Paul had to say about this:

*[64]For the weapons of our warfare are not carnal but mighty in God for pulling down strongholds, casting down arguments and every high thing that exalts itself against the knowledge of God, bringing every thought into captivity to the obedience of Christ, and being ready to punish all disobedience when your obedience is fulfilled.* **2 Corinthians 10:4 NKJV**

Oh yes, in order to *Do the Greater* and for God to establish us, we need to overcome the enemy of progress and every enemy that stands against us. I thank God that he has given us powerful weapons that are strong and mighty in defeating devils, demons, witchcraft, evil people and evil systems that are against our lives. We can destroy them one by one. Our weapons can track, nullify and destroy every weapon and position of the enemy.

We are not fighting because we want to fight. No, we are fighting for our lives, our success, our health, our finances, our businesses, our churches, and our children, friends and family. We are fighting to have peace and joy. We are fighting to bring transformation to our neighborhoods and nations. We are fighting for single parents, orphans and people without support. We are fighting for the rich who cannot find real love. We are fighting to conserve our environment. We are fighting until racism, discrimination, gender biases and marginalization come to an end. We are fighting for a better world of mutual respect, honor and dignity. We are fighting that the will of God prevails in our lives and in this world. So, we fight well. The word of God in us is powerful enough that we do not need to add anything to it.

I feel sorry for all the lost pastors, prophets and prayer people who join witchcraft and secret societies, who do animal and human sacrifices just to have power and perform miracles. They do not know God; neither do they know the power of God. They do not know that by the stripes of Jesus Christ, sicknesses and diseases can be healed and lives restored. They do not know that at the measure of the name of Jesus, demons submit and flee. If they knew God, they would never find inferior powers to make a name, earn money and buy things. God is sufficient all by Himself!

The Word of God is a weapon of attack. The blood of Jesus is a weapon. The name of Jesus Christ is a weapon. The Holy Spirit is more than a weapon. So why would any pastor, prophet or prayer person need power through voodoo, witchcraft or secret societies? Aha, I know the answer.

It is anxiousness, impatience, greed, arrogance and love of power. When things fill your eyes, you will lose your way to Jesus and run after things and people. Quite interestingly, when Jesus is in you, you will value the ministry, honor people, and serve them with the love of God. The way you will handle the people and things God entrusts to your care will be so different because you will do it out of love and service as unto God.

Unlike all this mess, we can use the spiritual weapons of our warfare to bring down bad arguments that want to disturb our peace and take people away from God. We can pull down anything that exalts itself higher than God or anything that tries to be God. We will even be able to control thoughts in our own minds and the minds of others through the power of the living God. All this will happen because we need to bring everything to the obedience of the lordship of Christ Jesus that all may know God.

The next thing I love about exercising our power in the Lord is that when our obedience is fulfilled in Christ Jesus, we can begin to judge the world by punishing every act of disobedience, especially the ones that come in our way. We can begin to preach peace in the troubled world; we can bring food to the hungry and give justice to those who deserve it and discipline all the perpetrators. We can expose all the liars, gossipers, imposters and pretenders and show the world who they are and punish them. Look, we have too much power and authority in the Lord, that when we start to utilize it properly, our communities will change and development will come.

It is my ardent prayer that the true believers in your area will arise and take charge of things so that God can manifest his *kingdom come.* God wants to move and do great things through you, but he is waiting for people like you and me to call him and take our proper place in society.

Are you going to shy away or are you going to take your stage and address the situation? We need to take the stage and give our best performance to the world. If you and I do not go out there to do our part, a lot of things will not be fine. We must overcome every force that stands in the way of justice and peace. We must overcome the vices in life and not let evil people have their way; we can defeat evil only if we can work together to promote good. We must fight evil; the evil we do not fight to overcome is the evil that taunts us and seeks to destroy us. I am not ready to die; I believe it is the same with you as well. If this is true, we need to team up to defeat wickedness in society by serious consistent affirmative action. Get ready. Evil is raging.

The Bible teaches us that the Word of God is alive and active. It is powerful. The Word of God is living, active and powerful; it breaks through souls and spirits, bone and marrow, and even knows what is in a person's heart. Wow, I need more of the Word of God in my life to be on top of things. Look at this:

> [65]*For the Word of God is living and powerful, and sharper than any two-edged sword, piercing even to the division of soul and spirit, and of joints and marrow, and is the discerner of the thoughts and intents of the heart. And there is no creature hidden from His sight, but all things are naked and open to the eyes of Him to whom we must give account.* **Hebrews 4:12-13 NKJV**

I want to emphasize that we serve the living God, and he is not a dead like the gods others serve. Our God is alive and well. Quite interestingly, other religions cannot dare talk about their gods as living gods; they do not have that luxury because their gods, or the chief representatives of those gods, are all dead and gone. We serve a living God; that is good news for all those who believe in the Lord Jesus Christ as their personal Lord and savior. Let me ask you: do you serve God?

Do you have any other gods? Or do you claim to have no god because you believe there is no God? If you do not have a god or you do not believe in the existence of God, please let me introduce my God to you. First things first: I serve a living God who is active and powerful. If you want the conservation, we will go on from here. As I pray about how to be established, it is my hope that you will be encouraged in your spirit to discover the power that is at work in all of us.

We need to use the Word of God against our adversary. The devil does not care about your name; it does not scare him. The truth is, I think you are more afraid of the devil than he cares about what your name is. I believe you and I know what evil looks like, the pains and sufferings it can bring. If you do not know what evil is, you will see it by watching television. But when Satan sees the name of Jesus Christ upon you, he is forced to bow because it is a powerful name. The name of Jesus Christ will make him flee from you. When you are in Christ and Christ is in you, your name can also become a problem, a great threat to the devil because of how much you serve the Lord.

One thing I love about the Word of God is that it is more than any spy agency in the world. It is better than all the governments of the world put together. It searches the hearts and intents of men; it brings about the concept of pre-crime, except that pre-crime looks at tendencies.

On the other hand, the Word of God sees what is behind every action, singular, plural, complex or mixed. It goes deep to the area of our soul and spirit and down to our biology, deep down into our bones and marrow to discover the secret upon secrets. While man is hiding things from neighbors on land, deep underground, in the waters and seas and up in the sky, all of them do not seem to care about finding out upon whose property they are hiding all their stuff. The funny part is that man hides in secret places or plain sight, not hiding from the one to whom all must give an account of our time in this world.

Because God is the creator all things known and yet to be discovered, we cannot hide anything from him; not in the darkness nor in daylight. God controls the spheres and states of gasses. He controls land, water and air and everything in it in the form of light, gas, solid and everything in between. I am simply trying to tell you that when you have the Word of God in you, he exposes deep and hidden things to you. Whether it is the secrets of the enemy, or things about your own life you need to know, or things that are relevant to others or, of course, insights into our specialties in life or spiritual things. God's Word can give us revelation about all things.

All we need to do is make sure we have the Word of God in us. It is living, active and powerful. It breaks through every barrier and detects all things; nothing can hide from God. With this being said, when we have the Word of God in us, we can see, arrest and punish anything that wants to get out of bounce. We can discipline any person, place or thing that wants to disturb our peaceful rule, steal from us, or try to destroy or kill us. We have the power and authority in the Word of God to deal with all such opposition. It is my prayer that you will possess the Word of God in your personal life and use it accordingly.

The Bible teaches us through the Prophet Jeremiah that his word in us is a battle ax. To put it in simple words, when we have the Word of God in us, we become battle ax in the hands of God to destroy the enemy. An ax has weight and is sharp, usually used to split wood or cut down trees. We, as the people of God, are battle axes in the hands of the living God to destroy the works of the enemy.

> [66] *"You are My battle-ax and weapons of war: For with you I will break the nation in pieces; with you I will destroy kingdoms; with you I will break in pieces the horse and its rider; with you I will break in pieces the chariot and its rider; with you also I will break in pieces man and woman; with you I will break in pieces old and you; with you I will break in pieces the young man and the maiden; with you also I will break in pieces the shepherd and his flock; with you I will break in pieces the farmer and his yoke of oxen; and with you I will break in pieces governors and rulers.* **Jeremiah 51:20 NKJV**

I want you to answer this simple question. Who are you in the hands of the living God – a loser or a powerful winner? If what God says to the Prophet Jeremiah is true about you and me, why are we crying, whining and complaining all day about the devil and the evil people when we are supposed to fight them and overcome them with the Word of God? Huh, I think I know the answer: we are not what we are supposed to be in the Lord to become the strong people and winners God has called us to be. That is why we become victims of circumstance and victims of the constant attacks of the devil. Some people do not even get a break to rest; one evil befalls them as soon as the other ends – even at times the evil things happening to them can pile up.

I believe that when God looks at us from heaven he becomes so disappointed that his battle axes and weapons of war do not fight and suffer violence at the hands of an inferior enemy. I really feel sad in the place of God. We are the battle ax of God and weapons of war. In our world today, we all know how deadly terrorists and suicide bombers are; well, God says that we can become more deadly to the devil than any human invention. We can defeat the devil in any battle because we are superior and have heavy-grade weapons.

When nations and their armies of wickedness rage against us, we can defeat them. From one rank to the other of every evil unimaginable, God says we can defeat all of them from those on the ground to the water and in the air and everything in between; we can defeat them. We can defeat evil systems plotted by the rich and mighty, by kings, queens and their governors. Oh, how much I wish we knew what power and authority we carry as the people of God! We have power that is alive, active and forceful in neutralizing every attack of the devil and we stand ready to mount an instant counter-attack. We need to make preemptive strikes so that the devil does not even have a chance to come at us.

With all this power and authority in the Lord, what are the people of God doing when evil is climbing at the doors of the church? Do we just blame it on the end-times or are we consumed with self-aggrandizement or just ignorant? What is our problem? We must wake up because evil is changing good traditions and introducing cultures that will affect our daily lives, children and the future of the church and the nations of the earth. Why does the church seem comfortable inside when the world outside is falling apart? Let the people of God arise, repent and pray for the nations to find God. We have a unique role to play in the line-up of things. There are statements to be made to the devil and all wicked people about changing old boundaries and good traditions that kept our civilization strong and gave us healthy, thriving societies. We must tell the instigators that they cannot get their way in polluting society and get away with it; no, we must arise and set things in order before it is too late.

You are the battle ax of God. You are deadly to the enemy. You are weapons of war, not just one pistol, rifle or sword; you are weapons of war. You are a terrific opponent that cannot be defeated. Once you stand up on your feet, because of how powerful and strong you are, the enemy must bow and ask for peace terms or be obliterated. You have weapons that are not of this world, so the enemy can never figure them out. You are the neutralizer. You create calm but yet instill fear. Do not ever overlook who you are in the Lord. When you appear, demons and witches must beg and hide or die. You are somebody in the hand of the mighty God who created all things – living and nonliving, known, yet to discover and unknown. You have weapons of war, use them to protect and wall off all the enemies that want to destroy you and your society.

The Bible teaches us through the Prophet Daniel that we can do great exploits for the Lord. I am ready to take charge of my life, family and society. I am ready to bring honor to my life, my family and my nation.

Maybe you are like me and we have been hiding in the corner when we are supposed to be on the stage of life performing our gifts; but now, the sleep is over, I am standing up to do something before time passes over me. I refuse to be one of those old men and women who lives in regret in their old age when they reminisce about their lives and see that they have done nothing good compared to their peers.

I refuse that a thousand times; that can never be me living in regret in my old age. I will live a meaningful and rewarding life so that when I am very old, I will look back and be glad about the legacy I am leaving behind. If you have not started working on what you want people to remember you for and what to leave behind for your family, you better start doing something today.

*⁶⁷Those who do wickedly against the covenant he shall corrupt with flattery; but the people who know their God shall be strong, and carry out great exploits. And those of the people who understand shall instruct many; yet for many days they shall by the sword and flame, by captivity and plundering. Now when they fall, they shall be aided with a little help; but many shall join with them by intrigue. And some of those of understanding shall fall, to refine them, purify them, and make them white, until the time of the end; because it is still for the appointed time.* **Daniel 11:32-35 NIV**

Let me recapture the first part for you. We are reminded or informed that there are those who go against good traditions, and against the plan of God in our lives and for the world. For those wicked people, God himself shall corrupt them and flatter them. Yet for those who know God as their Lord and savior, they will be strong and do great exploits for the kingdom of God. They will collect bounties after winning battles on every front. I am so filled with joy and excitement to know that there are great exploits to collect. There are souls to win, the oppressed to be delivered and those bound to be set free. Education can overtake ignorance and discipline can overcome arrogance and laziness.

Peace can replace war and self-development, opportunity and capacity building can replace hunger, diseases and poverty. When the strength of those who know their God is manifested and they begin to do great exploits, peace and tranquility will reign and chaos will vanish.

I am so excited to see the people of God everywhere taking their proper place in society in spite of the challenges they encounter to overcome evil and its proponents. We must arise from our sleep and do something before it is too late.

JAMES C. NYEMAH

When the people of God embark on projects to advance society, there will be battles to fight. The good news is, for whoever stands against our mission, then they will be a trophy to win. We will not just win; we will take the plunder.

When God's people come together, there is no force, system or person who can stand us. When the people of God take their proper place, in spite of some pains to endure, we shall overcome every terror that threatens our peace and freedom.

Our world today is so chaotic because good people sit around, do nothing and see evil grow. When will we get up, or do you want to see some mass shooting in your neighborhood, your kids' school, your church, business or social event before you come to yourself? Do you really want your friends and family to die in a plane crash, or at some airport, or at the hands of terrorists and suicide bombers before you wake up? It is about time that all of us, for the sake of life, peace and freedom, forget our differences and work in unison to defeat the emerging evil. Wake up, be strong and do great exploits. The world is watching; and of course, God is watching all of us.

There are some people who are afraid of pain and suffering. Oh well, all I can tell you is that for almost every good thing we have in life, we must sacrifice for it. To stop wickedness and evil in our society is not an easy thing. The people who do bad things will come after you when you try to save others and destroy their wickedness; but regardless of what attacks they mount and the pains you feel, press forward until you win.

The Lord is with you in all you do. As a matter of fact, the passage you just read said that at times God uses pain and suffering to refine us, purify us and make us white and blameless before him. When you face trials and temptations in your attempt to do good, do not let that bother you too much or let it make you quit.

We will have challenges in life and in our calling, but this does not mean that we should quit because of problems. When we have challenges in life, it tells us that there is something good about us and God is giving us something powerful to do. What troubles you? What do you see wrong in your area, in your life, business and ministry? God is working in us to bring about his perfect plan for our lives, families and society. Do not let problems scare you away, because those who overcome are called champions.

## f. MAKE THE DIFFERENCE NOW, NOT NEXT TIME

Do something with your life today. You can make a difference today; not tomorrow, not later. No time for empty promises; it is time for fulfillment. This is no time to joke; it is time to work. Others are going ahead of you; it is your time to act now. I am here to tell you that you can make a difference in your life today; others are doing great things and you can do something today, too. What failures have you had in your life so far? Are you not tired of them? What losses have you encountered that brought you shame and disgrace? Do you still want to be like that? Who has walked away from you and said you were *"good for nothing"* and *"useless"*? Do not let wicked people have their way in your life; wake up and do something today. If you were sleeping; please wake up. If you were acting like you are dead, get up to do something because you are still alive. Stop acting lazy and wake up to do something meaningful.

Everybody can make a difference in our world today. You can do something and I can do something. All of us can do something; something that will make a difference. Whether you do big things or small things, all of us can make a difference. I want to make a difference and I know that you would like to do great things, too. We need to work on our dreams in life and ask the Lord to help us fulfill our visions. Our vision for life varies, but the most important thing is that you are doing something to fulfill your purpose in life. Whatever that thing is in your heart to do that will solve a problem and relieve pain and suffering, whether you are inventing or improving something, I want to encourage you to do your part today.

I do not know if you have people in your life who do not believe that something good can come out of you, or people who cheated you of some things or opportunities; it really does not have to make you refrain from pressing on in life. There were times in my life when people, including my family members, looked down upon me and made me lose some opportunities. They felt somehow that I was not qualified to partake in certain things that all of us as family were supposed to enjoy. My name was left out. They found all the useless reasons they could give and told me how I did not fit certain criteria, even though I really stood for the family in care and support. They did not know that darkness can never quench light. They tried, but the God inside me was just too good to let me suffer without helping me. Today, without boasting and being proud, I am humble to tell you that the Lord is doing some great things in me and I am so grateful. To be frank, I do better than some of them today.

Looking back at things now, I realize that it does not matter who believed that I could do something good or not. I had to believe in myself, trust God and work on my calling in life. Regardless of your background, race, education, socio-economic status or connections, each one of us can make a difference. There are some little things that you and I need to pay attention to if we want to do something better in life. Before you start jumping up and down, warming up and running out to save the world, let us examine a few things about you and your passion and calling in life.

Let me make this simple for you to understand because I feel that some people are now listing big things they want to do but they do not have the resources. If you are like me and many people, with great ideas and no money, you need to really pay attention here. First things first: everything is not about money. The primary thing you need is an idea and the passion to fulfill it; so, take it easy. I know you have great things on your mind, but do not go that far yet.

Let us start with you organizing yourself properly. How much time do you spend on entertainment as opposed to educational things? Is television, video games and social networks like Facebook, Snapchat and Instagram taking up precious time away or are you the type who goes from house to house talking useless things or just cooking to eat all day? Are you in control of your time and your activities? Alright, tell me how you normally start your day and manage your daily activities. Are you asking me whether you should answer? Yes, answer me. Let us get it on; yes, you can say something now. Go ahead and say it out loud how you usually start your day and what you do daily. Take a look at how you run your day.

Do you have a plan or do you just wake up, go out and do whatsoever anybody tells you? Or are you the one just responding to things, but you do not have any plan for yourself? Please answer this last question for this session. Of the things you do from day to day, how do they connect to your vision and how do they help you fulfill your vision in life? Answering these little questions will help us examine our daily activities. Knowing how to properly manage your day is very essential to fulfilling your dreams in life. Whatever you do with each day is very important because days, as they go by, can turn into weeks, and weeks turn into months and years. Overlooking your daily activities will make you lose sight of the purpose in life and put you in the category of people with dreams but who are never able to fulfill them.

Let me be frank; this is especially for all the religious or Christian people out there. Spirituality alone without balancing reality using the natural order will not help you become what you need to become in life. A lot of religious people and Christians just want to fast and pray all day long without finding something to do that will give them something to eat, a place to lay their head and provide for their family. Even the Apostle James teaches us to properly use faith and works, for the proper application of these two will give us anything we desire from the Lord.

> [68]*Thus also faith by itself, if it does not have works, is dead.* **James 2:17 NKJV**

So while fasting and praying are good, the absence of work can hinder our prayers. We need to pray, express faith and work hard; that is how it should be. Whatever good things your hand finds to do, do it with all your might; give your best to that thing and trust God. I believe that when you do this, the Lord will help you. Jesus said about himself that,

> [69]*I must work the works of Him who sent me while it is day; the night is coming when no one can work.* **John 9:4 NKJV**

For the people who love procrastination, Jesus said that it is not a good thing. He said that He Himself had to work when it was still day because at night people do not work and the night is creeping in. This analogy is not referring to physical day and night alone because there are many people who work both day and night. The day here represents the time and opportunities we have when we can do things. Yet there come times when we are not able to do as we would like when sickness comes, or trouble, imprisonment or death. These things hinder us from working on our dreams in life; they represent the night. Therefore, while we still have time, health and ability, we need to do whatsoever we can to make a difference in the world. People are looking for people with great ideas to make things work well. What are you going to do?

Wherever you are today, I encourage you to begin to work on yourself and pursue your dream in life. I want you to know that if you do not work on your dreams, it will be hard to find others to work on them. If you are not careful, someone will attempt to take what you have and use it and nobody will know you. Whatever you have, properly register it and work on it. If you can work alone, just do it. If you need partners, start looking. No matter what you do, do not stop working on your dreams in life. That special thing God puts on the inside of you can give you worth, make money for you, give you recognition and make an impact. I believe you will be glad when you see the outcome of your own labor. God bless you.

# Part Six

## PART 6: ESTABLISH ME

    a.  Established Forever
    b.  Established in your Finances
    c. Your Children Shall be Established
    c. Requirements to be Established
    d.  God will Establish your Legacy

# ESTABLISH ME

I will not suffer all my life. I will make it. I will not see other people doing great things while my heart burns because of defeat and shame. I will not be living then have people forget about me because I have nothing good to offer. Ah, that cannot be my portion in life; I refuse it! My hard labor and trust in God will pay off; I will make it. I must make it. By the grace of God, I will make it somehow, no matter how long it takes. As a matter of fact, I am working hard right now so that things can work out very soon. I refuse to look at other people being well-established, living life, enjoying their families while I remain poor and suffer.

I do not want to read the news, watch television or go around looking at the success of other people, including people I know, while my life is not going anywhere. I will make it. If other people can go to school, learn and become somebody, I, too, will get there. If other people can start businesses and become very successful, then I, too, will make it.

If people can start organizations and companies that are doing quite well, I will do my own, too. If others in the ministry are progressing in the Lord, I refuse to be in a small church that cannot even pay its bills, much less compensate me as pastor year after year while others are doing great things for the Lord. If others are doing well, I must do better because we serve the same God. If the books, music, organizations, companies and inventions of others are helping others, giving them notoriety, making money, giving them a good life, my name must be at the top of that list!

If we have the same God as father, the Maker of the heavens and the earth, why should others enjoy life while I struggle year after year? Am I just good for "hand-me-downs" and donations and just live at the sympathy of others? No way; that cannot be my portion. I refuse to live just to survive instead of making great strides in life. I am good for something. I refuse to be a beggar at the doors of other people. I cannot just live borrowing money from people to pay bills. I cannot keep going from paycheck to paycheck or live in hard times every day. Things have to get better.

In the world we live in, a lot of people are selfish; they claim to have rights to their possessions and do not have to share with the poor or anyone else, for that matter. They feel they have earned their things and want everyone to earn theirs, too. They forget that the grounds are not even for everyone; they do not understand that some people have better opportunities than others do.

Once they have made it, they are not even interesting in helping others make it. They feel they should keep what they have and should not be obligated to give to anybody at all. Knowing that this mentality is commonly practiced in many places, why would anyone choose to live just to beg others to survive? I do not want to live at the mercy of others; I want to do something. I understand that when people give you things today, there are no guarantees that they will do that again and again; they will expect you to help yourself. That is why each one of us must desire deep within our hearts and souls something better for ourselves. We want to be established.

In this section, it is my ardent hope that you will grasp a deeper understanding in knowing that God has a special plan for your life: to prosper you, give you peace and longevity. I challenge you to take these words seriously as you have been doing through the previous chapters.

No matter what happens, I do not want to be poor, sick and broke forever. I must make it in life by the grace of God. I believe that you have a similar prayer, too.

All of us want to leave a legacy behind: something good for our families and something people will know us by for generations to come. As you read these following pages I want you to keep these things in mind. You can be established in life; let your prayer be, oh God, establish me today. Help me to make it in life. I am tired with how things are; I need change. Thank you now. Amen!

By the way, I want to ask you a few questions that I want you to remember as you read the rest of the book. It is about your death. Yes, even though I do not want you to die right now, keeping that in mind will help you change your course of action today and work hard if you want things to be different. Please bear with me because I understand that this is a sensitive subject; I will be as conscious as I can be.

Let us get into this. Okay, here we go. The day you die, will people be happy that you died or will they feel sad because they lost somebody important? Who do you really think will attend your funeral without complaining about the time because they want to leave? Did you just name some friends and family members? Are you really sure about them? Okay, let me ask you this one, too. What will you leave behind for your wife, husband or children? All right, let us take it a step further. What will your people, town, city, nation or world remember you for?

These questions are valid. The answers we give, if they are honest, will help you and I guide ourselves in making good decisions to move forward. I ask these questions to make you think about how well-established you need to be. Take your time and go over them if your answers were not so good. As you know, this is not a test to pass for grade; it is just something to help us examine our lives so that we can be our own judge to make all the necessary adjustments.

For your family and friends to feel sad about your loss and stay beside you during your funeral until they bury you, you have to mean something to them today. For you to leave something good behind for your wife, husband or children, you need to be established today, or at least start working on it. If you want your community, city, nation and world to miss you, mourn when you die, you have to become a person of substance.

For people to honor you and create awards, foundations and statues in your honor or name streets, buildings, cities and parks after you, you have to do something meaningful for your society today. While all these things are good, and we have seen people whom others have treated with such honor, we cannot become that unless we become established. It is my solemn prayer that you and I will work on our dreams to fulfill our purpose in life; the fulfillment of that will establish us in everything we do. Do something. There are a few points I want us to dig into; I believe that they will help us in our pursuit of becoming well-established and leaving a great legacy behind.

## a. ESTABLISHED FOREVER

The plan of God for our lives is not for us to suffer, be broke, poor and sick. God has something better in store for us. I refuse to struggle day after day just looking for food to eat and a place to sleep; no way! Seriously, that can never be my portion. God is not in the business to taunt us with a few things that we can see but never possess. Other people have cars, houses, money and a lot of things, yet some people cannot even find food to eat. Some people have things that can vanish after some time; that cannot be my portion. What God has in store for you and me is to establish us once and for all and move from one level to the other, making progress. In the lineup of things, God wants us to increase from one level to the other; not to remain stagnant or go down in obscurity.

Our desire to be established is once and for all; it is about going higher and higher and higher in the Lord and doing great things. We will not go below and become nothing when we obey God and walk with him. This is what the Bible said,

> [70]And I will establish My covenant between Me and you and your descendants after you in their generations, for an everlasting covenant, to be God to you and your descendants after you. **Genesis 17:7 NKJV**

God is saying to us that he will establish his covenant with us; that covenant includes our children and descendants for generations to come. The covenant of God for us and our children is more than a high-yielding savings account. It is much like a trust fund and annuities that pay heavenly dividends over time; and I love that. It is an everlasting covenant to bless us and make us be a blessing to the world. Because of the covenant of God that guarantees health, wealth and longevity, we can become somebody great and be a blessing to the world. I love this very much. It is like God telling us that he wants to give us something good that will help us have reason to live and laugh.

On the outlook of things, it does not seem to be much; it just says that God will establish an everlasting covenant with us and our children to be our God. So, what does this really mean? Well, I will help you understand the magnitude of this covenant.

When you understand the depth of this covenant, you will begin to fix up things with God to ensure that you are properly listed and included in the covenant. God says he will be our God. Alright, let's say we accept the offer; what do we really get?

To answer that question, let us first of all look a little bit into who God is. God is the creator and sustainer of all things: both things seen and unseen. At his spoken word, our universe, in all it intricacies, came into existence. When he spoke, his word reverberated in emptiness to create galaxies, large and small, far and near, and all their contents like the sun, moon, stars, black holes, dark matter and even things we humans have not yet discovered. God made everything.

Quite interestingly, if God made everything, it shows that God knows how to create balance in his creation to keep things going the way they are. We see harmony between both living and nonliving things. We see things that make life possible and things that enhance life.

God knows how to run things. He is good in physics, chemistry, biology, geology and many other disciplines that maintain things for smooth operation. God is good security and, of course, a very good leader. So, what does it mean again for God to be God to us and our children and the generations that follow? It means that because God made us and put us in charge of things, we have his creative power, sustaining power and leadership power. It tells us that we do not have to worry about provisions because God cares for his creation; he provides food for every living creature.

This means that we can have direct access to God to work a unique relationship with him; a relationship that strengthens our standing with him. When God becomes our God, we do not have to fight a lot of battles; most of the battles belong to the Lord because we are his children. I could go on and on about the magnificent glory and splendor of God in creation and how he keeps order, but I would love to bring it down to your understanding before I bore you with all this.

When God becomes our God, he puts us in charge of things, guides us through life's journey and helps us discover our purpose to reach our destiny. When God is our God, he gives us more than daily bread and shelter. He gives us provisions for a lifetime and teaches us how to make more supplies.

I am so glad that I accepted the offer of God to make him my God so my children can have true security and staunch leadership in all aspects of life. When you give God a chance to be your God, your circumstances are bound to change; for God is a God of change. There is a certain peace and joy that words become inadequate to express, a peace that comes from knowing God personally. This, I must be quick to say, has nothing to do with religiosity; it is about carving a unique relationship with God that only takes us higher and higher in everything we undertake.

Do not just come to God and let him in because of the benefits, as that will sound selfish; it will appear that you do not actually desire a relationship. Meanwhile, it will interest you to know that making God your God will give you many benefits that your life will become a walking testimony. It will become inspirational stories that, when told, will inspire others to greatness. When God becomes your God, it casts away all fears, doubts and other insecurities; in place of that negativity, you get confidence, peace, joy and assurance. You will not have to worry because now you know that you have a God who is bigger than all your problems.

I know some smart people are already asking me that if all this is true, why do we see believers suffer? Thank you for your curiosity. I, too, asked that question. But let me tell you, it is not that you might not face problems, but God will lead you through every single one of them and make you an overcomer. For every problem that comes your way, when you take it to God in prayer and apply faith, it will become another testimony, a story about the goodness of God that you will be glad to tell others.

I want to encourage you today, as you desire to be established and become somebody in life, to accept the offer of God and make this journey easier. I believe with my whole heart that God will not disappoint you. By the way, when you ask around to check out if God is worthy of all this talk, you will discover that God is bigger than what people say. He is bigger and better! Let God in today with your heart and soul; I guarantee that you will discover a certain peace you do not have words to describe.

## b. ESTABLISHED IN YOUR FINANCES

God has a great plan for the money you need to use your entire life. His plan is simple: prosper you in all things! I love this very much because I know quite well what it means to be broke until you cannot afford to buy water to drink or have gas in your car to go to work. I know how painful it is to see things you want but you do not have the money to buy them. I know how terrible it is to see your friends go to fine places like restaurants, movies and concerts but you cannot go because you are so broke. I know what it means when you are so broke that you do not have any fitting clothes to wear; oh yes, I know that quite well.

I have seen some wonderful students with brains and great potential drop out of school because there is no money to pay their tuition and other fees. Even some of the students who managed to pay their tuition and fees barely have clothes to wear and good food to eat; they struggle a lot. I have seen a lot of men lose respect just because they do not have money; it is a sad reality. I have seen a lot of women, especially single moms, struggle to raise their kids. They barely have fitting clothes to wear and struggle to put gas in their cars to go to work. Life is not really easy for anybody who does not have money and other resources to live. It is very painful.

I must be frank to tell you that this does not even scratch the surface of the impact of poverty around the world. If some people in America and other developed countries are poor, homeless and destitute, what can I say about people in Africa, Indonesia, South America, India, etc.? Poverty should be something the whole world needs to fight; country by country, region by region, city by city; people need to wage a serious war on poverty and initiate programs that will empower people and reduce or eradicate poverty.

We need to devise ways to combat poverty. Poverty should never be used by any government or people to control others; that is just sick. Yet the truth remains, there are governments and other people around the world who actively encourage poverty. They want to live better than other people do. When things are better for people, development comes, education flourishes, advancement in arts, science and technology come into play and business grows.

When this happens, the eyes of people become open and they will soon realize that other people have been stealing from them; they will put stop to it. Because the evil scavengers around the world living good lives cannot continue when people take charge of their land and improve, they would rather find means to keep them in bondage. They seem to be willing to give aid and loans that will keep people in bondage than to give them the capital they need for development. They just want to give *hand-me-downs* just to look good and fill their evening news with sad images of the poor and suffering in Africa and other places after they make millions and billions out of those people. Open your eyes; not everyone is really good.

There are people who use the plight of the poor to take advantage of them and plunder their lands by stealing important things in the land, like timber, gold, diamonds, bauxite, oil and many fine minerals. Look at Africa; it is a black man's continent, yet some whites have laid claims to countries and rule everything in them; they suffer the natives, steal their land and subject them to modern day slavery and cruelty.

I do not know about any city in America or another developed country where Africans or any other nationality control a state or region where the citizens of that land have no voice. Then here is my question: if this cannot happen in other places, why does it plague Africa? They make plantations that encourage modern-day slavery and pay the people a penny on the dollar or less. They do not care about developing the land; all they do is to take and take and take.

Quite interestingly, it is the developed countries that mostly plunder the land of the poor; they do things to other people that they will not allow anyone else to do to them. This is so sickening. They go to the extent of poking their noses into the affairs of other people when they do not properly take care of their own. It is shameful to see homeless people lying around street corners in America and other developed countries with pain in their eyes, begging for food and money in the rich man's country. They do not seem to care for people; all they care about is money and power. People everywhere need to be very careful about these gluttons who come around pretending to be friends and business partners, because a lot of them are really not what they say they are.

They sit in secret places and plan how to destabilize regions so that they can take advantage of the situation to plunder the land. They affect governments, politics and business. They use their military as a force of oppression to subdue anyone who opposes their evil, dominant rule. People of sound mind need to put on their thinking caps and be careful with the amount of aid without development funds given to them. People need to be very careful with these blue- and white-collar criminals and underground terrorists who pretend to be friends. They are savage wolves in sheep's clothing, ready to take from where they did not sow. I mention this to say that poverty is something many big-name people and governments use to control people. If you are a leader in your country or wherever, please open your eyes and look beyond things as they appear. Some images can deceive people; be very careful. Our world is so different these days. Enemies do not come as enemies; they wear nice suits and come as business partners and investors; beware.

People need to be empowered, and not stay in line for rations. The good news is that God wants to bless you and me so much that the day we tell people stories when things were bad, they will not believe us because of how much we will have. It is the plan of God to make you somebody special. God wants to bless you and make your name great, but we must walk with God and obey his instructions.

I want you to pay attention as we go through this section. It has some nuggets that, when applied accordingly, will change your thoughts and your finances; and, thus, change your life. Give me your attention, please. The first thing I want to tell you is to stop looking at others to help you before you can stand. You have what it takes on the inside to make it in life. All you need is to work on that thing that is in your heart and see how your faith, hard work and prayer will attract people to see, talk, touch and invest! Let me tell you, the people will not come to invest in what they are not seeing; no, they will only come to invest in what you currently offer that assures them of something better on the way. Therefore, stop running after people to get assistance before you use your head and apply your mind.

I hope this is not too difficult for you to understand; okay, let me make it simple. Before I break this down, let me tell you what Dr. Nasir Siddiki of Wisdom Ministries in Tulsa, Oklahoma – USA told my church the first time he visited us. He said that we need to work with God if we want any miracles in our lives. God has the SUPER that is in SUPERNATURAL. So if we want the SUPERNATURAL, we must first do the NATURAL and then God will add the SUPER to give us the SUPERNATURAL! I love this so much. We are not supposed to sit down, whine, talk, complain or just eat and sleep when we can do something. The world is changing every day; we must do something that will help us succeed.

It does not matter what we do, though it must be legal; we must do something in the direction of our calling in life. Whatever that thing is for you, begin to pursue it. Let me remind you, the Bible says that we will eat from the sweat of our brow. So what good thing are you doing and sweating for? That thing is supposed to bless you; it will prosper only if you work on it, pray about it and apply your mind. Do not listen to naysayers and doubters; they will become people who promote your name and product when you succeed tomorrow. Some of them will even become your customers or employers, if not partners; so do not worry about what people tell you. Follow your dreams and God will prosper you.

*[71] "By the sweat of your brow you will eat your food until you return to the ground, since from it you were taken; for dust you are and to dust you will return."* **Genesis 3:19 NKJV**

There are a lot of people who do not want to work or like to work; they just want things from other people. They choose to be a liability to family, friends and the society when nothing is wrong with them. There is nothing wrong with them physically or medically, but they are just lazy. Some people develop the habit of chronic begging, they are not sick in any way, but they do not want to work. There are others who are just flat out lazy and greedy; all they want to do all day is to eat, watch TV, play video games, hang around and many times poke their noses in other people business. No, that is not good at all. The Scripture above said that by the sweat of our brow we shall eat and live in the land. We need to find something to do and the Lord will bless the work of our hands.

If we want for God to establish us, then we must get ready to work. We have to give God something to bless; but if you and I refuse to have a seed, then how can God bless the seed to grow and bear fruit in thirties, sixties and hundreds? We want increase, but increase comes from existent things either by addition, multiplication or by exponents; either way, it stems from what we have. God expects us to have something already because of the life he has given us to live. Whether you have many things or not, it does not matter; but each one must bring something before the Lord so that he can bless it to multiply. Listen to this example of faith and work in action. When the two come together, we get answers; we get miracles.

> *12 Then Isaac sowed in that land, and reaped in the same year a hundredfold; and the Lord blessed him. 13 The man began to prosper, and continued prospering until he became very prosperous; 14 for he had possessions of flocks and possessions of herds and a great number of servants. So the Philistines envied him.* **Genesis 26:12-14 NKJV**

Let me tell you the story behind this, there is famine in the land of Canaan, a place where Isaac lived. Isaac prayed to God and asked for direction. As of before, when there was famine in the land, his father Abraham went to Egypt, in Africa, to fetch food and they survived the hunger. So Isaac wanted to go to Egypt to find food as well; but when he prayed, God told him not to go to Egypt this time but to go to Gerar, a city of the Philistines. It was then there that the Lord spoke to him to sow in the land, to plant a farm and he did.

When Isaac obeyed the Lord and planted a farm and sowed in the land of Gerar, in that same year God blessed him and he harvested hundred times the amount of crop he sowed. Isaac had a hundred times in crop and cattle and servants until his wealth made his host king to drive him out of town. King Abimelech of Philistines, in Gerar, told him to leave town because he was richer and more powerful. He saw the economic strength and manpower of Isaac as a threat to his kingdom. Isaac had to leave town because God prospered him as a refugee looking for food in a strange land to the extent his riches and servants intimidated the king of the land! If I was Isaac what would I care; I would simply move to the next town or city with all my money, people and things and settle there.

There are few things I want us to consider here as we talk about the need for God to establish us. According to the story, his condition pushed him to begin to make decisions; instead of leaving God out, he turn to God in prayer to seek direction. I do not know what you are going through that is pushing you to make decisions, but I encourage you not to rush and jump to conclusions; seek the face of the Lord first. His leading is the best for you right now and for the future.

The other thing to look at is this, Isaac wanted to go to Egypt because when famine came the last time, his father Abraham went to Egypt. Let me be quick to tell you, do not do things because other people did them and things worked for them, even if they are your family or friends. You are not them and things may not be exactly the same; and besides, the plan of God for your life may be different. Do not ever try to be a sneaky copycat; be distinguished. It does not matter who your supporter or role model is, do not just do things because they did them this way or that way, even if the people you are following are your family and close friends. Ask God for directions concerning your situation in prayer; the Lord will answer.

Now pay close attention to this; Isaac prayed and God answered him. His answer was not to go to Egypt but to go to Gerar in Philistia. A lot of people want God to lead them and bless them; but sadly, inasmuch as they pray and seek the face of God, they do not want to obey the voice of God. If you are not willing to obey the leadership of God, why waste your time to pray, fast and do charity because you want a certain miracle? It is a total waste of time to do all that when we will despise the voice of the Lord to guide us. Instead of whining, complaining and nagging about this strange place, Isaac trusted God and moved his family to Gerar.

Let me ask you: what directions did God give you after you prayed to him about your situation? Did you follow the voice of God or you chose to do your own thing? Did you do your own thing because you thought what the Lord asked you to do is somewhat inconvenient? Whenever we do not obey the leading of God in our particular situations, we stall our own progress and cause much harm unnecessarily.

This, I tell you, is a very sad thing. Why will we waste our precious time to pray, seek the face of God, even sometimes give sacrificially when we will not follow through and obey God? When we do this, we rob God of his glory and cheat ourselves of the joy we should have had when we receive good things from God.

Our brother Isaac obeyed the voice of the Lord and sowed seeds in the land; when he did, he reaped a hundredfold. The harvest lies in the seeds you sold. The quality, not necessarily the quantity, of the seeds you sow determines your harvest. While it is good to sow more seeds, it is far better to sow quality seeds that will move the heart of God. If you are sowing seeds in someone's life, give them something that will move them, something that will surprise them. You can start with your parents or some special people who support you in life.

Isaac could have acted like he knew too much and told God that his seeds were the last ones he had to feed his family. I have seen a lot of selfish people who use their family when they do not want to help anybody; do not be like that. So why will he leave certainty for uncertainty when he did not have a real guarantee that the seeds will grow much less bear any good fruit? This is where many of us miss the mark.

Instead of obeying the voice of the Lord, we want to reason out everything and try to fit it in our limited way of understanding when the ways of the Lord are so far from our ways? Besides, God does not have to explain every detail of his plan to us before he can bless us at any given time. When God speaks, all we have to do is obey his voice and follow his plan.

When I look back at my own life, I wish I had just listened to God instead of listening to people who gave me so-called *"good advice"* but yet led me astray and betrayed me. Because of my own cleverness, I have lost some precious people and things; I wanted to figure out everything before acting and totally forgot that God is not obligated to explain any details to me.

While God expected me to listen to him and obey his voice, I was expecting God to give me the details so I could make an informed decision. I did not get such answers from God; to my loss, I missed some great opportunities in life. It is just better to trust God and obey him. I learned this lesson the hard way. Please do not let a similar thing happen to you.

Isaac obeyed God and sowed in the land of Gerar; and when he did, the Lord bless him greatly in wealth. He became mightier than the king of the Philistines and the people of Gerar. Let me tell you something about this, it does not matter whether you are an immigrant or citizen of any place, when you listen to the voice of God and obey him, he will bless you greatly. We need to learn this from our brother Isaac and take the words of God seriously. Whatever God tells you and I is sufficient to produce the miracles in our lives that we long for. Do not ever overlook the voice of the Lord or despise his leadership. God works in mysterious ways and he can do anything at any time to bless you.

There are things we need to invest in. Whether it is a savings account, trust fund, annuities or stock and bonds or some business; whatever that thing is, when God directs us, we need to hear the voice and God and move quickly. We need to make the most of every opportunity that comes our way; we must understand that good things do not come knocking over and over always.

There are other times when we need to do sacrificial giving. When those times come, we need to seize the opportunity and give to those in need, give out of gratitude or give forward because we believe God for some miracles.

Isaac believed the word of God, obeyed the instructions, never went to Egypt, stayed in Gerar and sowed in the land. Because of his obedience the Lord blessed him so much so that his wealth intimidated the king. As the story goes, the king later realized that this guy was too blessed and could not be dashed down just like that, so he made a peace treaty with him. His wealth gave him goods, money and people that were quite noticeable.

God blessed Isaac until he became prosperous and prosperous until the man became very prosperous. In modern day English, we would say that the man became stinking rich – a multi-billionaire!

If God did that for hungry Isaac who was a stranger, an immigrant who had to settle in Gerar of Philistia, why not you and I? The qualifications for the blessings of God are not that difficult as we think; they are as simple as trusting and obeying God. Yet to our loss, we do not always do that though it means good for us.

I do not know what you are asking God to do to establish you; for me, I have just few things on mind. Is it your invention, product, business, organization, talent or church? Whatever that thing is, God is the one who gave it to you in the first place; so he wants to use that gift, talent and ability to bless your life, your family and the world.

As you pursue your purpose in life, you need to work on the vision God has given you. As you work and pray, have faith and put your mind to work. When you do that, God will bless you mightily. I want to encourage you to trust the leadership of God and obey him as I do too. Let us be like Isaac and do this together so other people can read about us tomorrow and watch us in the news and later watch our movies. I think that will be a cool thing.

## c. YOUR CHILDREN SHALL BE ESTABLISHED

The plan of God to prosper us is not just for us alone, it extends to our children and generations tocome. God knows that it is by grace that we can pass seventy years of age; that is why he put things in place that our children can enjoy from us. We took some time to talk about Isaac. But who was Isaac? Isaac was the long awaited promised son to Abraham and Sarah; a son of their old age, the son through whom the nations will be blessed. Yes, it was that Isaac we were talking about.

God promised Abraham and his wife a son; a son that would continue their legacy. Today I pray that your children will be great people that will continue your legacy. It does not matter if they are not up to speed right now, I pray that the God of miracles will locate them, touch them and bring them back to their senses because they need to continue your legacy. If you do not have kids, I pray that the people after you who manage your affairs will properly execute your orders when you are gone.

This is what the Scriptures say,

> [73] *Then God said: "No, Sarah your wife shall bear you a son, and you shall call his name Isaac; I will establish My covenant with him for an everlasting covenant, and with his descendants after him.* **Genesis 17:19 NKJV**

149

I want to say this to you: you will not just be looking at other people stuff and wonder what time something good will happen for you too. If you do not have any good thing today, I pray that the Lord will speak to your life and make something happen. If you just do from hand to mouth, paycheck to paycheck, I pray that God will make you become distinguish. Wherever you find your life in the lineup of things and want to be established, I pray that the God of miracles will open doors for you.

Music and Charity Ambassador Kanvee Gaines Adams from Liberia sang a song in which she asked a daunting question saying, "God, if you are blessing other people, what about me?" I join Kanvee to ask too, so what about me and what happen to you? What about me God when you are blessing other people? Am I the worst sinner so I do not get any blessings or help in life? Yet I know some people who morally do worse things than I, yet they seemed to be ahead in life; so I do not think it is all about my sins being too much or unforgiveable. I know your love can cover me and redeem me from any awful state. I trust you.

It burns my heart at times to see other people enjoying life while others live in abject poverty without any assistance. As patient minded as I am, it gets to me at times and I too ask God how come others are going ahead in life, buying houses, cars, enjoying family dinners at high-end restaurants, showcasing thriving businesses, organizations, and churches while I am struggling from month to month? What are they doing that I am not doing or what do they know that I do not know that is suffering me?

I really hate to see children suffer without proper care because their parents cannot afford it. I hate to see women, whether single, married or single moms suffer without any help in life. I really hate to see men suffer without end; it is like their lives have lost substance. The lack of money and things is a serious problem. If we as adults and parents do not have it, how can we cater to our families, much less give our children any inheritance? There would be no legacy for them to further; they would have to start from scratch. A lot of children struggle in life because their parents left nothing behind for them to start with.

It is my ardent hope that all of us will work with God to become established in life and leave something good for our kids. If my grandparents and parents suffer, I refuse to follow their path; I will have money and do great things. My kids cannot even live the life I live today; things have to be better and much easier for them because of the foundations I am laying for them today. All of us need to work on our dreams and passions for life so that God can bless the work our hands and establish us. When you are I are established in our lifetime, our children will even begin to live and enjoy the good life before we can depart this world.

Over and over I see that God cares for our children. God said he will provide for our children. We have this assurance in the Lord, that though we need to apply wisdom in bringing kids in this world and not just be having kids we cannot afford to support, God has a plan to care for our children.

*[74]So then, don't be afraid. I will provide for you and your children." And he reassured them and spoke kindly to them.* **Genesis 50:21 NIV**

We do not need to be afraid because we can trust in the promise of the Lord to provide for our children. Yet in simple wisdom, bringing kids into this world when we ourselves cannot find food to eat is not the wisest thing to do. Kids need good care; so before you go to do the stuff that can get women pregnant, you need to think twice about the potential consequences of the choice you and your partner is about to make. When pregnancy comes, people then have two choices whether to keep it or get rid of it. When you are not ready to have kids, please do not get pregnant only to kill the kids; for they are precious unto the

Lord regardless of their manner of conception, deliverance, care, and upbringing. Children were never met to be put up for adoption because they need their real parents to love and care for them. Such things at times come up when parents cannot afford to support their babies or refuse the babies; either way, it creates some issues in the lives of the kids, when they are in good homes.

> [75] *Build cities for your women and children, and pens for your flock, but do what you have promised."* **Numbers 32:24 NIV**

There is a special place in the heart of God for women and children, and that is why He instructed men to build cities for the women and children to live. Women and children need to be in a safe and secure place and given all the necessities of life to live good and comfortable lives. In simple words, God was instructing the men to establish something good for the women and children so that they will not suffer in life.

We need to make room and build a decent environment wherein our women and children can live in peace and tranquility. We need to provide shelter, food, clothing, education, job opportunities, development and a bright future for our people.

Men have a great responsibility to work hard and build cities for the women and children. The cities represent all the good things we need to make available so that our women and children can live meaningful lives as often as possible. We fulfill this calling of God when we take the time to love our women and children and properly care and provide for them. Men who do not love their women and children do not provide for them most of the time, if they do so, they do it because they have to and the relationship is absent.

*[76]Only be careful, and watch yourselves closely so that you do not forget the things your eyes have seen or let them fade from your heart as long as you live. Teach them to your children and their children after them.*
**Deuteronomy 4:9 NIV**

There are good things about you and me that we need to pass down to our children so they do not have to *"reinvent the wheels"*. We need to teach them properly with patience until they master the art of any discipline required. We need to teach them about love for self, love for family and the delicate issue of sex and love. We should take it to the next level and teach them leadership by example that first starts with us.

The children need to be educated to guarantee a better life tomorrow. We need to teach them good morals and how to represent us and present themselves before anybody. Our world today is competitive; we need to prepare them to have the edge and leverage.

We must understand that the world is not a plain field where people play fair; no, there are cheaters and strong opposition and usurpers and a lot of wicked people out there. They include those who want to steal, kill and destroy us. This is quite necessary for our children because we do not want others to squander our hard earn wealth we left with them without them enjoying life and building on it. As we do this, we need to teach the children about God and His impact on society; acceptance or denial of God has serious consequences that could affect them and their own children as well.

Let us work hard and teach all the good things to our children to lay the foundations for their lives to have balance. Whatever we teach them, plus what they themselves have acquired, is what they will present to their kids. If we want our generations to love God, respect family, be educated, and advance is life, we must begin to teach our children today.

## d. REQUIREMENTS TO BE ESTABLISHED

Many things in life have requirements. For example, to enter college, students are expected to meet certain requirements. There are requirements for admission which includes proper documentation of your past and current academic records, tuition, fees, and acceptance of the school's regulations. To operate a motor vehicle in the United States of America, every applicant must pass a written test and physical road test. If you do not pass the written test, you cannot take the road test; if you do not pass the road test, you cannot obtain a driver's license. This is a requirement everyone who wants to be a driver must meet.

In the same manner, even though all of us are the children of God and have equal access to Him, to be truly blessed and fully established in the Lord has a price tag. We live in a world today wherein everything costs something; nothing seems to be for nothing. There are stories and conditions attached to things in life. Only the people who fulfill the requirements can be a part of that thing, even though there are cheaters around.

I want to dig in the below passage because it has great revelations that will help us to understand the requirements of being established in the Lord. God loves us and wants to bless us; that is so true but yet many of us are so far from that.

By discovering our wrongdoing and understanding how God works to bless us, we will be able to know, do and finally become what God intended us to be in the beginning as people who are blessed, and multiply, who can fill the earth, subdue any opposition and exert proper dominion. I am so anxious to see that the Lord is making me become; and for you, your testimony will be great and surprising to people.

*[77] "Thus says the LORD of hosts: 'If you will walk in My ways, And if you will keep My command, Then you shall also judge My house, And likewise have charge of My courts; I will give you places to walk Among these who stand here.* **Zechariah 3:7 NKJV**

I love this passage because it is full of instructions. The Bible teaches us not to despise instructions because they are beneficiary for life. Whatever we want to do or become in life, we must learn the art of that thing and master the unique details only those who diligently search can discover.

*[78]Listen to my instruction and be wise; do not disregard it.* **Proverbs 8:33 NIV**

There is something quite interesting that happens to children from the same parents. Some of the children respect and honor their parents, love instructions, go to school, pay attention, learn something good and become somebody great.

On the other hand, there can be some other children in the same family who are rebellious from the start or learn it along the way. They disrespect their parents, fight, break stuff and do not like to go to school.

Instead of sitting in classroom to learn, they jump class to go somewhere else and many times, get in trouble with the law; yet all the kids are from the same house. While some children get involve with teenage pregnancy, drugs, alcohol and gangs, other kids are learning, working hard and making great strides in life.

They go from court to court and sometimes go to jail or prison. What is the difference? It is as simple as obedience, following instructions.

In my recent book, **Born To Take Charge**, I wrote that,

[79] *"Obedience calls for respect, agreement, conformity, and honor. To obey someone is to submit to their leadership. We obey people and people obey us. When we do this, we can live and work together in spite of our difference."* **Born To Take Charge - Chapter 4: Obedience Brings Victory**

To walk with God, we must begin to obey him. If we do not want to agree with God and obey Him, then we will not walk in His ways. This is what the Prophet Amos said, [80]*Can two walk together, unless they are agreed?* **Amos 3:3 NKJV**

God wants to bless us and establish us; but we must learn to agree with God for our own miracles! In my position as pastor it frustrates me a lot to see people who would refuse simple instructions from the Lord for their conditions. They enjoy me telling them stories from the Bible about people who obeyed God, even under harsh circumstances, and got their miracles.

They really enjoy it when I tell them about the miracles of God in the lives of other people, even in the church and in ministry as a whole. They love to hear testimonies about the goodness of God in the lives of other people; yet sadly for them, they do not want to do what it takes like the others who received answers.

People like these keep shouting "Amen, Amen and Hallelujah" for other people miracles, yet nothing works for them. I can wonder, when will we be happy because the Lord has answered their prayers too. This is a serious problem I see wherever I go; many people want miracles, but they do not want to obey the instructions given that make miracles possible. They seem to forget or perhaps are ignorant of the fact that heaven has principles and miracles have conditions.

The writer of Proverbs advised us not to disregard instruction but to be wise and listen to instruction. Zachariah, the Prophet, spoke the Word of God to the people and called everyone to walk in the ways of God and follow His commands.

When we do this, then we can experience the goodness of God in many ways. God is really interested in our total wellbeing; not just to give us rations. I hate begging for things. I really hate standing in line for things; I only do so, if I must really do. I want to be able to have free access and grab what I want than to wait in long lines. If God has a plan to put me in charge of things, I will do it.

*[81]Thus says the LORD of hosts: 'If you will walk in My ways, And if you will keep My command, Then you shall also judge My house, And likewise have charge of My courts; I will give you places to walk Among these who stand here.* **Zechariah 3:7 NKJV**

To our greatest loss and frustration to God, many people do not want to listen to Him, obey Him, or walk in his ways; thus living substandard lives than what God planned for them. God has a great plan for you and me; but the only way we will experience that is when we learn how to obey God and walk with him. I find it very difficult to work with people who do not seem to care about what we do; it is just hard. Notwithstanding, I find it quite exhilarating to work with anyone who has a passion for the job; it can be so much fun.

I love the above passage in Zechariah so much because it lays the grounds for our blessings; and the key component is obedience. We must do our part to keep God's words and walk in his ways. It is a kind of obedience that goes beyond regular religious duties like going to church and giving offerings. While all that is good, but it goes beyond the walls of the church to the marketplace of life. God wants us to obey him and walk in ways concerning community, education, business, politics, science, development and everything that pertains to life.

The call of God is not just for church people alone; no, but rather it extends to whoever will respond so that through them God would do great things to bless his people everywhere. Regardless of our backgrounds such as place of birth, ethnicity, education, age, size or financial status, when we listen to God, obey him and walk in his ways, he can bless our lives and establish us. We can go from obscurity in becoming prominent figures the world will forever remember. We need to do it the way God has commanded and things will go well with us; all of us. When we do this, all of us will be happy.

When we do this, we obligate God to do his part to make us judges over his houses, put us in charge of his courts, and of course, give us places to stand like others who do great things.

Every day God is looking for people just like you and I to work in them and through them to do great things. Remember that song of Liberia's Charity Ambassador of Music, Kanvee Adams, that asks the question about our place, our position as God is blessing others with well-paying jobs, college degrees, cars, houses, business, big ministries and money. What about you and I? What happen to us that we cannot see the glory of God manifest in our lives to get a break from suffering just to enjoy small? Aha, this kind of suffering is terrible. I need a break to enjoy the good life too. I am tired of this mess. I must come out and do great things too.

I know sometimes people wonder about what time people will listen to them and do things for them instead of serving people throughout their lives. They too would love to be a charge of something and somebody. They want somebody to make reports to them, sign checks or give approvals; they just want to be up there to serve in higher and perhaps, prestigious positions. Who told you the servant cannot be a master one day? Nobody said the student cannot become the teacher someday; as a matter of fact, it happens always. So then what about you and I too? Are we left over or what?

You need to be in charge of something, something that will bring you worth, make you money, make you serve in a greater capacity and help others. I need to be in charge of preparing more leaders for tomorrow and instill good character, discipline and teach leadership principles in the church and the marketplace. All of us need to be well-established and leave something good behind for our children, and even their generations to come. Oh no, this is not being greedy or asking for too much; there are people in our society, because of one or few well-to-do person or people in their families, they have a great start in life. Do you have money put away in CDs, trust funds, stocks, bonds and annuities that collects interests over time and grows bigger and bigger year after year? Oh yes, others do that and they are very happy with the results because they are earning great interests on their investments. What about you? Because of this, according to the will of that well-to-do relative, family members listed can get their share of the monies or properties according to the conditions set by that person. I tell you this to understand that what I am talking about concerning the blessings of God to establish us is not a joking matter; it is serious business.

When we walk in the ways of God and obey his commands, we will be rulers of his house. I love this part right here because God's house is not some kind of tiny thing with no space, simple studio or one bed, one bath deal; no, it is a house with many mansions. This is what Jesus told the people,

[82] *"Let not your heart be troubled; you believe in God, and believe also in Me. In my Father's house are many mansions; if it were not so, I would have to you. I go to prepare a place for you, I will come again and receive you to myself; that where I am, that where you may be also.* **John 14:1-4 NKJV**

I want you to know that in God's house there are many mansions; not just tight spaces. I want to also let you know that God intended for you and I to be in charge of those mansions in his house. All the mansions contain things specific to life that would organize, create, invent, nurture and promote life, health, church, community, technology, science and different innovations to make our world a better place for us and our children. Quite interestingly, this thing has little or nothing to do with religion; it credits faith and the pursuit of one's purpose in life.

I think I am confusing some religious people who like to think that God only intended to bless only those who go to church and give offerings; no, that is limited information. God has principles, natural and spiritual principles; some of them intertwine with each other. So if the church going Christian does not follow the natural principles of God that have spiritual components, that Christian will not benefit from the rewards of those who apply them diligently. On the one hand, there are those who apply the physical principles but ignore the spiritual dynamics; they may do well in the physical world, but yet their soul has no peace and they often die as miserable people.

We need to understand that the rooms in God's houses are mansions fully equipped for us to operate our plot in life and do everything we need to do before we die. Each one of those mansions assigned to you and I have all the contacts you need to fulfill your calling in life. It contains the names and contact information all the people you need to work with in reaching your goal. I mean it includes all your partners, employee, friends and fellow teammates to do the job.

The list also contains specific information about all your competitors and opposition and how to handle them. It contains information about their soft spots and detail information on how to use that to your advantage. In a special place inside the mansions lies the safe and its combination codes holding all the different currencies of the money you need to do the job, enjoy family, save for tomorrow, start new innovations and to continue your legacy. All the money you need is right there.

By the way, before I forget, I must tell you that there is a folder in one of the cabinets that is well labeled that holds information about your office space, warehouses, production centers, service centers and showrooms, whichever is necessary for you. All that information is right in there; so you do not need to look any further or go to the wrong addresses to start.

God has a plan and it is a great plan for you and me. All we have to do is walk in his ways, follow his commands and we will be in charge of his houses, his courts and have a place among the others that are settled. Let me dig into these three classifications of things: house, courts, and those over there. Bear with me as I go carefully to help you better comprehend this matter.

There are some people God seems to give some special ability or gift to create and invent things that can be so useful to the world. Their creation gives them notoriety, fame, money and people at their command. The things they do are in high demand and they create jobs, settle some problems in the marketplace for goods and services, and put them in the position to do so much for humanity. These big boys and girls have empires, conglomerations that make them so much money; they are well settled. They are the folks God talks about when he said that he will give us a place among the people standing there. God already "*made*" them and "*settled*" them; so they have nothing to worry about except to find new ways to make their goods and services better. This is the last group; but the first class in reality. People in the category are very few.

The second class of people is those who control rooms or mansions in God's house. Like the first class, they have money, people and things at their command; but greatly vary in size, quantity and magnitude. Just like in the time when

God bless man and told them to be fruitful, multiply; but he also said to fill the earth. While to be fruitful, multiply and fill the earth talks about increase, but there is a great difference I can explain in the form of a fruit tree. To bear fruit, if I have a mango tree, I can expect some fruits in its season.

To multiply, I have to have more than one mango tree bearing so many fruits; but if I want to fill the earth, I need to have mango farms big enough to meet local, regional, national and even international demands! That is the difference between allowing God to settle you by giving you and place among those standing there and ruling over his house, or its mansions. People like these are not that many, though larger in number than the first class.

Now let me talk about the third class, which is actually measured as the first group of people here. You and I know, there is a big difference between a house and the courtyard of that house; it is not the same. To have a court or courtyard, you need a house, but you can have a house without a court or courtyard.

While other people are inventors and big name leaders, and even as others have money, people and things at their command, not everyone is like that; there are others who seem not to fit that category. If you were to put them in the first group, they will almost freeze to death on stage because they will simply be too overwhelmed to perform. They cannot stand the amount of money available, the number of people to lead and goods and services to manage. They just cannot handle that.

Being in the second class is a dream for them; but just like the first class, the reality behind that dream is something they can only dream about but they do not seem to have what it takes to deal with the tension. So, the only place they can perform smoothly is to handle matters of the courts or courtyard. This wonderful class of people is the vast majority of manpower in today's workforce.

They do well in different capacities to serve as employees, but not as employers. No matter what their title is, besides those of them that are ready to jump to the second class like presidents and CEOs of companies and other organizations, they feel very happy with their jobs and do not want to deal with the stress of being up there.

Now let me be quick to say this, whether you find yourself in group three or two, you can work with God to satisfy you just where you are, or you can show God that you are prepared to handle your own uplifting and ask him to take you to the other step. There is no statute of limitations is the kingdom of God; it is only subject to our desire to walk with God and obey his commands. I want to also tell you that as people can move upwards, so can people come downwards as well; it is left with each one of us to determine our own fate in life. We can agree to work with God to go up or disregard God and choose a path downwards; it is our choice, our decision.

Zechariah, the prophet, told the people that God wants to make all of us to be up there to stand in the place where he places those who are greatly ahead. The same way God lifted them up, he wants to lift us up too, only if we will walk in his ways and keep his commands.

[83] *"Thus says the LORD of hosts: 'If you will walk in My ways, And if you will keep My command, Then you shall also judge My house, And likewise have charge of My courts; I will give you places to walk Among these who stand here.* **Zechariah 3:7 NKJV**

I want you to join me from today and hereafter that you and I will learn to walk with God and keep his commands so that he can make us judges of his house, his courts and be among those standing there that he already settled. I do not like where I am right now to be my final position, no way. I want us to work with God so he can give us some fresh start and make us move from one level to another. I'm ready; I hope you are as well.

## e. GOD WILL ESTABLISH YOUR LEGACY

God wants the good work we do to continue so that others can build on it tomorrow. Think about the journey of the telephone. From the first old buggy stuff, to rotary phones, from there to touchtone phones, and on to hand-held phones and onwards to mobile phones; and now today we have the sleekest touch-screen mobile phones in all their variations and capabilities from Samsung, Apple and Blackberry with countless applications! From the first telephone to the sophisticated phones we have today, telephones are still being developed as a powerful tool of communication, work and of course, fun.

It is in his divine plan that even our children and trusted people can continue our legacy so that our name and good work will not be forgotten. God made a good promise to King David to continue his legacy; it is my prayer that our legacies will continue through our children or through our stewards.

*[84]And your house and your kingdom shall be established forever before you. Your throne shall be established forever."* **2 Samuel 7:16 NKJV**

God made a covenant with David as he started his kingship in Israel and assured him that his kingdom would be established forever. God told David that both his house and kingdom will be established forever. I love it so much because, not only will his kingdom be established, but his house will be established too. Like in the case of David, God has a great plan to establish us in our home, in the marketplace or in the ministry. I have come to understand that God cares so much about our business after we go. While we are here, God wants us to be established privately and publicly; get ready.

You are I have a platform, an office and a throne upon which we need to operate; and God wants to ensure that things continue to go on after we leave this world. When you know that God wants to continue what you will leave behind, it should put you in the position to better work on whatever we do today to prepare for tomorrow and leave a great legacy behind.

From one passage to the other in the Bible, God speaks about increase, massive increase for us and our children. This is to say that God wants us to be prominent figures in society, known by what we do; people who have stood the test of time and are well settled. It really does not matter what each one does, all that is important is to put our body, soul and spirit in it and for the hand of the Lord to bless it. Here are few Scriptures that speak about the increase from God for us and our children.

*[85]May the* LORD *cause you to flourish, both you and your children.* **Psalm 115:14 NIV**

This is a solemn prayer that we need to pray for our family, friends, church members, teammates, co-workers and neighbors. We need to pray for everyone around us that the Lord will cause them to flourish in all good things; not just for them alone, but also for their children.

God has made a promise to us; a promise that we can count on. This promise is good for us and our children, and also for our generations to come. I love this so much.

*[86]The promise is for you and your children and for all who are far off – for all whom the Lord our God will call.* **Acts 2:39 NIV**

What I love about this passage is that God is not selfish to bless only a particular group of people, but rather his blessings are for everyone who calls on him. Regardless of your circumstances, you, too, can enjoy the good life. When the blessings of God open over your life, it does not have a shortage; it multiplies many times over.

> [87]*May the LORD, you God of your ancestors, increase you a thousand times and bless you as he has promised*!
> **Deuteronomy 1:11 NIV**

I pray that God will bless you a thousand times so that your hard work will pay off. I know that God is a good and faithful God; he will do what he said in his word concerning us. Let us put all other things aside and work with God so he can fully establish us to become blessed so much so that our children after us will not have to suffer in any way. God wants to make your name and my name great now and in times to come.

If they can name cities, buildings, foundations, streets and organizations after people, my brother and sister, I pray that you and I will be so established that we will be in high demand to receive honorariums all over the world. It does not have to be limited to your country or where you live now; people can honor you in different parts of the world because of who God is going to make you become. I am so curious to see what organizations, buildings, streets and even statues will bear my name! I will be looking around for your own too; this thing is so powerful that I am just excited about what is about to happen to you and to me.

No matter who you are and where you are, God can bless you and make your name great. It is my ardent hope and prayer that God will establish you. Look, I know what is means to live in lack; just looking at things you cannot afford. I know what it means not to have a working vehicle and to endure cold winters and hot summers at bus stops or train stations.

I know what it means to see nice things that you cannot buy. I know that it hurts to see other couples going to the movies, nice restaurants, games and concerts but all you can afford is McDonalds and cheap Mexican food. It hurts to see your children not having nice things to wear. I know what it means for the best clothes in your closet to look like something people can wear to do yard work. I understand those pains.

I can say like the Americans say, *"I've been there, done that, and gotten the t-shirt."* Yes, I know what it means to have long, bitter days and sad nights because of lack; it is quite terrible. Poverty, non-achievement and misery shall not be your portion forever; the Lord will deliver you from every bondage. Work with God to make a new you; let God make you someone great who will become the new talk of the town. I can see that, in your obedience, God is going to lift you up and you will go from one level to the next.

# Part Seven

## PART 7: PERSONAL DEVELOPMENT

a. People Management
b. Money Management
c. Discipline
d. Honesty and Humility
e. Strong Leadership

# PERSONAL DEVELOPMENT

There are few more nuggets I would like to give you before I close here. Something tells me that I have to give you this before I can go any further. I believe they will help you to prepare better as you work on your dreams and visions. Bear with me as I give you five points to help you in your journey to become established.

These few things will prepare you so that when your moment comes you will be ready to grab every opportunity. A lot of people missed good opportunities because they were not prepared or qualify. Do not let that happen to you. Good things do not come knocking over and over again. There are about 7 billion people in the world today; and the number is increasing daily. So if heaven shines on you and give you something good to lift you up and make you somebody, you need to cease the moment and make the most of it. Get ready to learn, stretch yourself, and sacrifice for what you believe in. If others are out there doing big things, you can make it too. Get ready today; prepare yourself before you miss your moment.

## a. PEOPLE MANAGEMENT

If you are to become what you want to do in life, you have to learn the art of managing people. But I must tell you, things and money seem somewhat easier to deal with than people.

In fact, if you are not careful, people will make you lose things and money and other people. People are difficult to deal with; oh yes, I know. At the age of nineteen, I was responsible for a family of twenty-five and now today I pastor few churches and collaborate with other pastors, ministries, organizations and government officials to do my work.

And, the truth is, even for the good of the very people you want to help, some of them will always come against you, though you are working for their good. You have to learn how to handle such issues.

Some people are aggressive and arrogant; they want you to do things their way or else, they will not comply. You need to learn how to deal with such ruthless people. There are some people who are flat out mean and selfish; they just want everything for themselves.

Get ready to balance your integrity before they pull you into greed and selfishness, less you destroy the purpose of your mission. Some people are boastful; they are full of it. They like to talk big, and even sometimes talk beyond their capability; they just like to boast and even lie about things they do not have.

Be mindful of such people before they make your heart fill with pride. There are some people who are creepy and others are lazy; you need to be a person and integrity and work your vision.

I say all these to tell you that you need to master the art of dealing with people because the success of your dreams, vision and aspirations in life depends how you relate to people. Do not just use people as means to an end, no; you must value people and give them the respect due them, even if do not agree with them. You need people to lead, to work with as partners, as team mates, as affiliates, and as employees. Take time how you deal with people because you need everyone you can get to fulfill you mission in life.

## b. MONEY MANAGEMENT

As you become establish and the blessings of God is flowing your life, your ministry, your business and family, you will have to learn how to use money properly. Money can be tricky; improper use of it is commonplace. Some people have kill others, cheated them, marginalized them all because of money. Those who have it have divided gender and racial lines because of money. Parents have killed their children for money; and children have killed their parents because of money. Friends have betrayed and killed one another because of money. Some business owners and employers have cheated and killed their employees and customers because of money.

Even in love relationships, couples, girlfriends and boyfriends have cheated, cheated and killed one another for the sake of money; so be very careful with money.

I want to be clear here: I am not saying that because people have used wrong motives to do evil because of money so do not acquire money or that you should go empty your wallets, houses and bank accounts and throw your money away; no, not that at all! On the contrary, we need money to pay for goods and services. We must learn how to handle money before the love of money create in us the evil seed of greed, betrayal, murder, using people like animals and treated them with all sorts of evil and disrespect. This is why we need to learn the art of handling money, whether big or small. If you and I cannot be honest with small amounts of money, why would anyone put us in charge of big amounts of money? It will not work.

For many things in life, we need money; there are times beyond the necessities of a place to live, transportation, food and security, we need money for business and investment. Yet in the midst of all these, we need to set something aside for fun and entertainment; there are times we need to take a break from work and enjoy the fruit of our labor with family, friends and some very special people.

I can see that God is about to do great things in your life that requires money, huge amounts of money. Because of this, you need to learn how to be honest, have integrity, and give account whenever it is required of you. You need to know how to spend money, pay bills on time, avoid late fees, trade, invest, save, make profit and leave for fun. This is the right time now to acquire all skills necessary to handle money.

If you do not know how to deal with money, money will put you in serious problem. Money will climb in your head and you will disrespect people; pride will fill your heart and you will begin to value money more than people. If you have not handle plenty money before, this is a better time to learn how to deal with money by learning how to budget and plan.

Money is sweet and has power; but letting money to climb in your head will be the worst mistake in your life. It can make people lose their humanity and turn into rich sick bastards that use money to commit heinous crimes to hurt masses of people yet hide beyond bribes so they will not face persecution.

As you deal with money, be focus on your mission in life; but no matter how much money you possess in life, do not forget to give to God what belongs to him and never stop doing charity. You must remember where you came from and that others are still below you that need help; you could be a helping hand to others to alleviate poverty, pain and suffering for others today.

## c. DISCIPLINE

Everyone need to master the art of discipline in life to be morally sound and decent people. We need to learn how to treat others with dignity and respect, even if do not agree with them. We need to learn how to control ourselves, whether in public or private. Do not be the lose man or woman out there who is just everywhere; learn to put yourself in order. We need to learn how to carry ourselves so that our appearance, talk and position will be something that others respect.

Even though they say that we should not judge a book as a cover, but as an author I know how important the cover of a book is, especially if you want people to pick it up in a bookstore full of hundreds of books. Before anyone can know about how sweet and nice you are, sadly, they look at your outfit first.

Many people are judged wrongly to be some kind of way simply because of their looks; some outfits we wear have certain associations, so be careful not to be placed in a wrong category because of your outfit. I do not want you to miss any good opportunity because your outfit disqualify you; dress accordingly in a way that represents the class of people or business you interact with.

We need to put our emotions in check before our feelings, which could be wrong sometimes, lead us to make rash decisions we will regret tomorrow. Control you temper or learn to initiate conversations.

While some people can get emotional and talk too much than necessary; there are others whose silence is making them fail in life. Talk when you need to talk; but remember to be quiet when time demands it too. Control your anger, jealousy and talk; please learn to put your emotions in check. Treat life as an important business deal you cannot afford to miss.

The other thing is that you need to master the art of the trade, business or organization you are dealing with. Educate yourself and invest in it in every way possible so you can be ready to answer questions and make declarations when you are asked. Do not be unprepared to perform in your area whenever you are called upon because you do not know who may be watching you. Learn about that thing and fight to be the best you can be. I want you to become the gold standard; it is the measurement stick of excellence. Be the point of reference and the expert that others will consult in your area in life.

## d. HONESTY AND HUMILITY

I love to be around people who are honest and humble. Whether they are family, friends, team mates, church members, or business associates, it is always a great thing to have honest and humble people. On the other hand, our world today has a lot of people who are dishonest, selfish and greedy; such people have a proud spirit and a few of them are rude too. This is not good at all. It is not fair to cheat others in anything we do in life. But I want to be quick to tell you that there are so many people today that are not honest; they just want something for themselves, even if it means they will steal from you, destroy you or even kill you.

[88] *"Do nothing out of selfish ambition or vain conceit. Rather, in humility value others above yourselves."* **Philippians 2:3 NIV**

There are people in our families, among our friends and in the workplace that are not fair; be careful with them before you become one of their victims. As you are going up in life, you must learn how to deal with them before they wreck your life. Unlike the evil of dishonesty, God challenges us to treat one another with fairness.

[89] *"Do to others as you would have them do to you."* **Luke 6:31 NIV**

Our world today is dying because of the lack of honest and humble leaders; you can begin to fill the gap today by being honest, fair and humble. We do not need to cheat others of what rightfully belongs to them. Let is remember the Golden Rule that demands us to treat others with fairness.

God does not love people who are proud and full of bigotry; no, but rather, God loves people who are humble. So all of us need to be humble and put aside our pride and ego that is driving us in tantrum just like little kids. We are mature now so we need to act like adults.

*"Be completely humble and gentle; be patient, bearing with one another in love."* **Ephesians 4:2 NIV**

As God is blessing you, do not allow pride to enter in you. It is like a cancer that destroys from the inside out; beware!

[90] *"When pride comes, then comes disgrace, but with humility comes wisdom."* **Proverbs 11:2 NIV**

Pride has a way to eat up people, do not let it happen to you. Pride brings disgrace, but humility gives wisdom. Do not let money and the people and things it brings turn you into something else; be the person you are and live your life. Treat everyone with respect. Be fair. Humble yourself and the Lord will lift you up in due time.

### e. STRONG LEADERSHIP

You and I were made to lead people, things and places. If you do not lead, someone or something will lead you; and that will be a shame to you and your family. Each person has his or her own platform upon which to operate; do not fight over another person's stage – go make your own stage. It is so sad to see many people who are called to be leaders join the line to follow the dreams of others when they have what it takes to lead in a particular area of life. Stop following people because there is another line forming behind you of people, things and places you are supposed to lead.

I know we must all start from somewhere; I know. Be an apprentice, a student to someone who knows the trade or art of what and who you are supposed to lead. And when you are fully trained, tested and ready to serve, take the stage and do what you know best and give people the best performance of your life in whatsoever you do.

If you are an inventor, give us your best product. If you are artist, bring us the best song, music and art work. If you are a scientist, we are waiting for your new discovery to help the world. If you are a medical doctor, people of dying of different kinds of diseases, what are you waiting for? Are you in sports and entertainment, you need to get out there and give us something exhilarating; nothing short of that!

What am I saying here? Whatever you are called to do in life, you need to do it by giving it your very best. But before you can get out there, learn the art of leading people, because you need them.

Learn how to control and manage money; your job requires you to make serious financial decisions. You will have things; you need to know how to acquire, maintain and replace. These are some of the things you need to get ready for. If you are not ready to deal with these, even though you are good, but your accountants, managers and consultants will eat all your money and throw you by the curbside as they go on looking for someone else to follow.

Let me be quick to say this, before you start leading your organization or family, you must learn to lead yourself first. If you do not know how to lead yourself, have financial management, honesty and respect, how can you lead others? Leadership calls for a strong heart to make decisions at times that goes against our emotions, you must be ready to deal with the tension before and after it brings. You must be prepared to handle the consequences of your decisions and own up to them, whether they are good or bad.

Leadership is not kiddie play; it is a serious matter. When you lead, others put the lives in your hand and trust you; you do not have to disappoint them like others do out there. When you put love for people above love for money and things, you will always have people that will make money for you and give you things. When you are above and well established, you need to learn to live like big people yet with a gentle spirit.

As you lead in your area, and as God is blessing your life, do not forget those who stood there with you when you did not have much and all those who helped you along the way. Leadership calls, take the stage.

I will see you on the other side in greatness.

I pray that this unit, coupled with other great resources

out there, will help you discover a life of purpose and leadership and show you the pathways to become established. I know that the Lord will bless you greatly; please remember to give me my little share. I love you.

# Editorial Reviews:

*"You will not read this book without giving serious thought to adding value to your relationship with God. The church has lost its way in many areas; but by reading this book, you are bound to reevaluate your walk with God. Not everything that glitters is gold. It's simple and straight forward."*
– **Rev. Joseph Bedah, Pastor – Bethel World Outreach, Phoenix, Arizona**

*"It is one thing to tell someone about something that will change his or her life, yet it is another thing to show the person how to implement it. This book does not only tell you, but it also shows you how to live an empowered life, you and all those connected to you. This is a great tool for ministers."*
**Rev. Sarah Kendema, Assistant Executive Director – Liberian Ministers Association of Minnesota**

*"Establish Me" is a book for believers; this book is for Christians with a firm desire to grow and be established in the faith. I am especially impressed by how Rev. Nyemah begins the book dealing with the issue of sin. Many Christians wallow in sin and still somehow expect the best of God without settling it. What I see deeply inherent in this book is that God establishes us on the basis of His word as we obey and serve Him. This book is a must read for any well-meaning Christian. Reading and comprehending the thoughts written therein will invigorate your thoughts and move you to action. I am especially blessed by this work. May God bless you and thank you Rev. Nyemah."*
– **Rev. Abilio V. Balboa, Resident Pastor and Assistant Missions Director - Philadelphia Church Ministries International**

*"In Establish Me, Rev. James Nyemah has shown the biblical basis for our lifting: God, who makes us global Christians and establishes our legacy as we serve God (and others) sacrificially. The sin that so easily entangles and destroys is what the author says we must put away to become new and attain our God-ordained levels. This is a great biblical insight for all who desire divine establishment!"*

**– Rev. Samuel K. Hinneh, Sr., Academic Dean, Liberia Assemblies of God Bible College**

# WHERE IS GOD?

James C. Nyemah

FORTE PUBLISHING

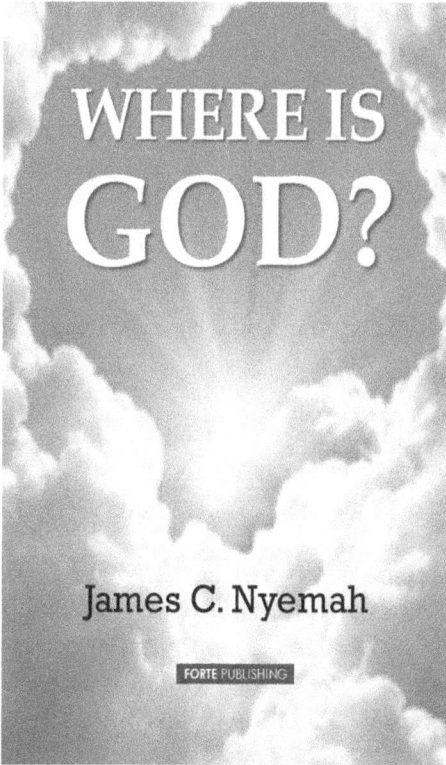

Read **"Where is God?"** - Finding the place of God in this world. When you find God, the journey in life becomes easier.

## Book Reviews:

*"I know James Nyemah. I know his heart for God, his deep concern for his people and his passion for living as a true disciple of Christ. If God's great purpose is to write a great story with our lives, then James Nyemah is a man through whom God has been creating a wonderful story of love and redemption. This book is a true reflection of James' life and character and the faithfulness of the God he serves."*
**- Dr. Maxie Burch, Chair, Division of Biblical Studies, Associate Professor of Biblical Studies - John Brown University**

*"I love the story and how you connected your life to it. The number of pages is perfect; it's also an easy read. I love the title. The title will draw people to want to read. You have done a great job. We pray God's blessings over the future of your ministry and this great book. Thanks."*
**- Pastor Dale Lane, Senior Executive Pastor, Phoenix First Assembly**

*"As a classmate of James, I was profoundly impacted by his faith and encouragement. This book does not avoid the harsh realities of living in a broken world, nor does it offer simplistic answers to important questions. It will encourage you and challenge you."*
- **Scott Savage, Pastor of Spiritual Formation, North Phoenix Baptist Church**

*"Pastor James Nyemah has done an insightful work on this book and I believe it will help every believer going through the storms in life to be hopeful."*
- **Pastor Ezekiel Ojo, Redeemed Church of God – Solid Rock Phoenix**

*"I like your book because of the many aspects you bring from Christian and non-Christian prospective. I will recommend pastors to read it and help our people change their minds and attitudes toward God."* - **Pastor Hypolite Kayenda-muntu, Senior Pastor of Ramah full Gospel church**

*"I have a great admiration for Rev. James C. Nyemah and the ministry God has given him. Filled with supernatural adventure, this timely book is essential reading especially for today's spiritual leaders."* - **Dr. Eric Minta, Christian Hope Ministries Int'l Church**

*And, also*

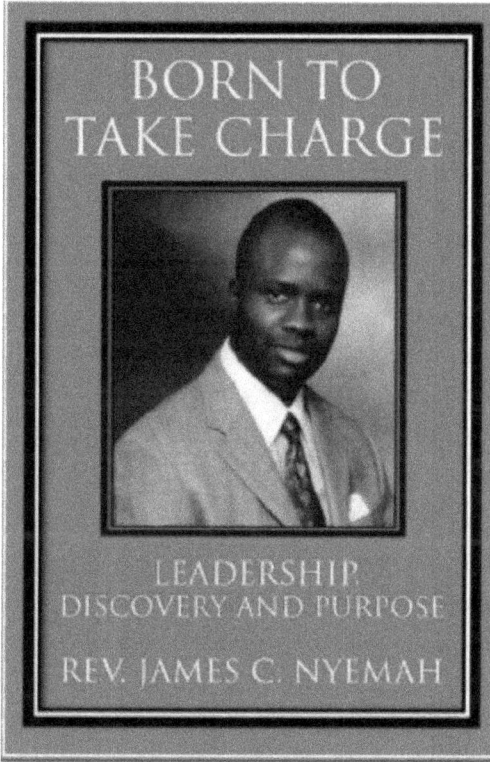

G̲et̲ "**BORN TO TAKE CHARGE**" – Leadership, Discovery & Purpose: Discover your purpose, reach your destiny.

## Book Reviews:

*"In plain language, Rev. James C. Nyemah challenges all of us to admit our human weaknesses, surrender to God, and through his enablement take charge of our lives to fulfill our God-ordained purposes. Take the chance to read the first page and you will not stop until you read the last sentence."*
- **Rev. Jimmy Kuoh – General Superintendent Emeritus, Assemblies of God, Liberia**


*"This book will touch many lives. The issues addressed are practically what many go through in life. Rev. James Nyemah generously shares outstanding insight and accumulated wisdom and provides a great apologetic for the Bible."*
- **Dr. Eric Minta – Christian Hope Ministries Int'l Church**

*"This is a very good book that young people and adults will benefit from. Take time to read it."*
- **Pastor Hypolite Kayenda-muntu – Ramah Full Gospel Church**

*"Pastor James Nyemah is a good example to follow. He is a leader among many. He united the African pastors in Arizona and organized prayer meetings for the Ebola Crisis in West Africa. We can see from this book no matter what happens in life, you are BORN TO TAKE CHARGE. Read the book and your life will never be the same."*
- **Pastor Antonio Kabamba – Jesus Promotion Church International**

*"This books tells us that we have been given a great gift from God. We must cherish it with ourselves and live a life with purpose. Each journey we take in life has a curve; it is up to each of us to seize every opportunity and make a difference."*
- **Ms. Henrietta Andersson – Executive Board Member, Liberia Association of Arizona**

*"There is no need to remain where you are. Being born proves that there is life. Let the life you live be the expressed purpose by which you were created. It is time to be taken from being a parked car along the curb of disappointment and failure and on to the highway of responsibility in the face of obstacles. Let this book move you to the place of fulfillment in Christ while you take your rightful place in leading others down the way the Almighty God will have them go."*
- **Pastor Lonny Du Four – Liberty Tabernacle Ministries**

*The Secret is out, so…*
Watch out for my next book:

# "Perfect Conditions"
– Creating perfect conditions for miracles.

May God create the condition that creates the condition that makes it necessary for your miracle!

# About The Author

Rev. James Nyemah is the Founder and Senior Pastor of Africa Faith Expressions, a church with branches in Phoenix, Arizona and Liberia.

He is a dynamic conference speaker conducting training in Liberia, touching thousands of pastors and community leaders. He is the author of **"Where is God?"** and **"Born To Take Charge".** He is a transformational leader with the heart of a servant.

Find out more about Rev. Nyemah at www.jamesnyemah.com today.

# References

[1] Romans 6: 15-16 Holy Bible, New International Version, 1982 by Thomas Nelson, INC, Nashville, Tennessee – USA

[2] Hebrews 12:1-2 Holy Bible, New International Version, 1982 by Thomas Nelson, INC, Nashville, Tennessee – USA

[3] I John 1: -9 Holy Bible, New International Version, 1982 by Thomas Nelson, INC, Nashville, Tennessee – USA

[4] Isaiah 1: 18-19 Holy Bible, New King James Version®. Copyright © 1982 by Thomas Nelson

[5] John 10:10 Holy Bible, New King James Version®. Copyright © 1982 by Thomas Nelson

[6] Isaiah 59:1-2 Holy Bible, New King James Version®. Copyright © 1982 by Thomas Nelson

[7] 1 SAMUEL 15:22, 28:15 & 19 Holy Bible, New King James Version®. Copyright © 1982 by Thomas Nelson

[8] Isaiah 1: 18-20 Holy Bible, New King James Version®. Copyright © 1982 by Thomas Nelson

[9] 2 Corinthians 5:17 Holy Bible, New King James Version®. Copyright © 1982 by Thomas Nelson

[10] Hebrews 12: 14 Holy Bible, New King James Version®. Copyright © 1982 by Thomas Nelson

[11] Hebrews 10:38 Holy Bible, New King James Version®. Copyright © 1982 by Thomas Nelson

[12] Matthew 19:26 Holy Bible, New King James Version®. Copyright © 1982 by Thomas Nelson

---

[13] Proverbs 3:5-8 Holy Bible, New International Version, 1982 by Thomas Nelson, INC, Nashville, Tennessee – USA

[14] John 3:3-5 Holy Bible, New King James Version®. Copyright © 1982 by Thomas Nelson

[15] Philippians 4: 17-19 Holy Bible, New King James Version®. Copyright © 1982 by Thomas Nelson

[16] Hebrews 13:17 - Holy Bible, New King James Version®. Copyright © 1982 by Thomas Nelson

[17] I Timothy 5: 17-18 Holy Bible, New King James Version®. Copyright © 1982 by Thomas Nelson

[18] Matthew 10:40-41 Holy Bible, New International Version, 1982 by Thomas Nelson, INC, Nashville, Tennessee – USA

[19] Matthew 10:41 Holy Bible, New King James Version®. Copyright © 1982 by Thomas Nelson

[20] Matthew 10:42 Holy Bible, New King James Version®. Copyright © 1982 by Thomas Nelson

[21] Matthew 20:1-15 Holy Bible, New King James Version®. Copyright © 1982 by Thomas Nelson

[22] Hebrews 11:6 Holy Bible, New King James Version®. Copyright © 1982 by Thomas Nelson

[23] Matthew 20:17-19 Holy Bible, New King James Version®. Copyright © 1982 by Thomas Nelson

[24] Matthew 20:20-23 Holy Bible, New King James Version®. Copyright © 1982 by Thomas Nelson

[25] Matthew 20:24-28 Holy Bible, New King James Version®. Copyright © 1982 by Thomas Nelson

[26] Philippians 2:12-16 Holy Bible, New King James Version®. Copyright © 1982 by Thomas Nelson

[27] Proverbs 18:16 Holy Bible, New King James Version®. Copyright © 1982 by Thomas Nelson

[28] Luke 19:30-35 Holy Bible, New International Version, 1982 by Thomas Nelson, INC, Nashville, Tennessee – USA

[29] Luke 19:30 Holy Bible, New International Version, 1982 by Thomas Nelson, INC, Nashville, Tennessee – USA

[30] Luke 19:31 Holy Bible, New International Version, 1982 by Thomas Nelson, INC, Nashville, Tennessee – USA

[31] Luke 19:31 Holy Bible, New International Version, 1982 by Thomas Nelson, INC, Nashville, Tennessee – USA

[32] Luke 19:32 Holy Bible, New International Version, 1982 by Thomas Nelson, INC, Nashville, Tennessee – USA

[33] Luke 19:33 Holy Bible, New International Version, 1982 by Thomas Nelson, INC, Nashville, Tennessee – USA

[34] Luke 19:34 Holy Bible, New International Version, 1982 by Thomas Nelson, INC, Nashville, Tennessee – USA

[35] Luke 19:35 Holy Bible, New International Version, 1982 by Thomas Nelson, INC, Nashville, Tennessee – USA

[36] I John 4:4 Holy Bible, New International Version, 1982 by Thomas Nelson, INC, Nashville, Tennessee – USA

[37] Acts 16:6-10 Holy Bible, New King James Version®. Copyright © 1982 by Thomas Nelson

[38] Matthew 28:18-20 Holy Bible, New International Version, 1982 by Thomas Nelson, INC, Nashville, Tennessee – USA

[39] Matthew 26: 36-28 Holy Bible, New King James Version®. Copyright © 1982 by Thomas Nelson

[40] John 10:10 Holy Bible, New International Version, 1982 by Thomas Nelson, INC, Nashville, Tennessee – USA

[41] Habakkuk 2:2-3 Holy Bible, New King James Version®. Copyright © 1982 by Thomas Nelson

[42] Matthew 26:39-41 Holy Bible, New King James Version®. Copyright © 1982 by Thomas Nelson

[43] Matthew 26:42-43 Holy Bible, New King James Version®. Copyright © 1982 by Thomas Nelson

[44] Matthew 26:38 Holy Bible, New King James Version®. Copyright © 1982 by Thomas Nelson

[45] Philippians 3:13-14 Holy Bible, New King James Version®. Copyright © 1982 by Thomas Nelson

[46] I John 4:4 Holy Bible, New International Version, 1982 by Thomas Nelson, INC, Nashville, Tennessee – USA

[47] John 10:10 Holy Bible, New King James Version®. Copyright © 1982 by Thomas Nelson

[48] Genesis 1: 28 Holy Bible, New King James Version®. Copyright © 1982 by Thomas Nelson

[49] I John 4:1 The ESV® Bible (The Holy Bible, English Standard Version®) copyright © 2001 by Crossway

[50] I John 4:2-3 The ESV® Bible (The Holy Bible, English Standard Version®) copyright © 2001 by Crossway

[51] I John 4: 1-3 The ESV® Bible (The Holy Bible, English Standard Version®) copyright © 2001 by Crossway

[52]Romans 8:14, 16 & 17 Holy Bible, New King James Version®. Copyright © 1982 by Thomas Nelson

[53] Mark 1:35 Holy Bible, New International Version, 1982 by Thomas Nelson, INC, Nashville, Tennessee – USA

[54] Luke 6:12 Holy Bible, New International Version, 1982 by Thomas Nelson, INC, Nashville, Tennessee – USA

[55] Psalm 36:4 Holy Bible, New Living Translation, copyright © 1996, 2004, 2015 by Tyndale House Foundation

[56] Genesis 1: 28 Holy Bible New King James Version®. Copyright © 1982 by Thomas Nelson

[57] Genesis 9:2 Holy Bible, New International Version, 1982 by Thomas Nelson, INC, Nashville, Tennessee – USA

[58] Matthew 22:36-40 Holy Bible, New International Version, 1982 by Thomas Nelson, INC, Nashville, Tennessee – USA

[59] Philippians 4:13 Holy Bible New King James Version®. Copyright © 1982 by Thomas Nelson

[60] Job 42:2 Holy Bible, New International Version, 1982 by Thomas Nelson, INC, Nashville, Tennessee – USA NIV

[61] Ecclesiastes 11:5 Holy Bible, New International Version, 1982 by Thomas Nelson, INC, Nashville, Tennessee – USA

[62] I John 4:4 Holy Bible, New International Version, 1982 by Thomas Nelson, INC, Nashville, Tennessee – USA

[63] Isaiah 54:17 Holy Bible New King James Version®. Copyright © 1982 by Thomas Nelson

[64] 2 Corinthians 10:4 Holy Bible New King James Version®. Copyright © 1982 by Thomas Nelson

[65] Hebrews 4:12-13 Holy Bible New King James Version®. Copyright © 1982 by Thomas Nelson

[66] Jeremiah 51:20 Holy Bible New King James Version®. Copyright © 1982 by Thomas Nelson

[67] Daniel 11:32-35 Holy Bible, New International Version, 1982 by Thomas Nelson, INC, Nashville, Tennessee – USA

[68] James 2:17 Holy Bible New King James Version®. Copyright © 1982 by Thomas Nelson

[69] John 9:4 Holy Bible New King James Version®. Copyright © 1982 by Thomas Nelson

[70] Genesis 17:7 Holy Bible New King James Version®. Copyright © 1982 by Thomas Nelson

[71] Genesis 3:19 Holy Bible New King James Version®. Copyright © 1982 by Thomas Nelson

[72] Genesis 26:12-14 Holy Bible New King James Version®. Copyright © 1982 by Thomas Nelson

[73] Genesis 17:19 Holy Bible New King James Version®. Copyright © 1982 by Thomas Nelson

[74] Genesis 50:21 Holy Bible, New International Version, 1982 by Thomas Nelson, INC, Nashville, Tennessee – USA

[75] Numbers 32:24 Holy Bible, New International Version, 1982 by Thomas Nelson, INC, Nashville, Tennessee – USA

[76] Deuteronomy 4:9 Holy Bible, New International Version, 1982 by Thomas Nelson, INC, Nashville, Tennessee – USA

[77] Zechariah 3:7 Holy Bible New King James Version®. Copyright © 1982 by Thomas Nelson

[78] Proverbs 8:33 Holy Bible, New International Version, 1982 by Thomas Nelson, INC, Nashville, Tennessee – USA

[79] Born To Take Charge - Chapter 4: Obedience Brings Victory, Page 47, Paragraph 1

[80] Amos 3:3 Holy Bible New King James Version®. Copyright © 1982 by Thomas Nelson

[81] Zechariah 3:7 Holy Bible New King James Version®. Copyright © 1982 by Thomas Nelson

[82] John 14:1-4 Holy Bible New King James Version®. Copyright © 1982 by Thomas Nelson

[83] Zechariah 3:7 Holy Bible New King James Version®. Copyright © 1982 by Thomas Nelson

[84] 2 Samuel 7:16 Holy Bible New King James Version®. Copyright © 1982 by Thomas Nelson

[85] Psalm 115:14 Holy Bible, New International Version, 1982 by Thomas Nelson, INC, Nashville, Tennessee – USA

[86] Acts 2:39 Holy Bible, New International Version, 1982 by Thomas Nelson, INC, Nashville, Tennessee – USA

[87] Deuteronomy 1:11 Holy Bible, New International Version, 1982 by Thomas Nelson, INC, Nashville, Tennessee – USA

[88] Philippians 2:3 Holy Bible, New International Version, 1982 by Thomas Nelson, INC, Nashville, Tennessee – USA

[89] Luke 6:31 Holy Bible, New International Version, 1982 by Thomas Nelson, INC, Nashville, Tennessee – USA

[90] Proverbs 11:2 Holy Bible, New International Version, 1982 by Thomas Nelson, INC, Nashville, Tennessee – USA

www.ingramcontent.com/pod-product-compliance
Lightning Source LLC
LaVergne TN
LVHW051513080426
835509LV00017B/2048